Walther Azzolini

Solution of restricted two-dimensional fabric cutting problem

AF138582

Walther Azzolini

Solution of restricted two-dimensional fabric cutting problem

LAP LAMBERT Academic Publishing

Impressum / Imprint

Bibliografische Information der Deutschen Nationalbibliothek: Die Deutsche Nationalbibliothek verzeichnet diese Publikation in der Deutschen Nationalbibliografie; detaillierte bibliografische Daten sind im Internet über http://dnb.d-nb.de abrufbar.
Alle in diesem Buch genannten Marken und Produktnamen unterliegen warenzeichen-, marken- oder patentrechtlichem Schutz bzw. sind Warenzeichen oder eingetragene Warenzeichen der jeweiligen Inhaber. Die Wiedergabe von Marken, Produktnamen, Gebrauchsnamen, Handelsnamen, Warenbezeichnungen u.s.w. in diesem Werk berechtigt auch ohne besondere Kennzeichnung nicht zu der Annahme, dass solche Namen im Sinne der Warenzeichen- und Markenschutzgesetzgebung als frei zu betrachten wären und daher von jedermann benutzt werden dürften.

Bibliographic information published by the Deutsche Nationalbibliothek: The Deutsche Nationalbibliothek lists this publication in the Deutsche Nationalbibliografie; detailed bibliographic data are available in the Internet at http://dnb.d-nb.de.
Any brand names and product names mentioned in this book are subject to trademark, brand or patent protection and are trademarks or registered trademarks of their respective holders. The use of brand names, product names, common names, trade names, product descriptions etc. even without a particular marking in this work is in no way to be construed to mean that such names may be regarded as unrestricted in respect of trademark and brand protection legislation and could thus be used by anyone.

Coverbild / Cover image: www.ingimage.com

Verlag / Publisher:
LAP LAMBERT Academic Publishing
ist ein Imprint der / is a trademark of
OmniScriptum GmbH & Co. KG
Heinrich-Böcking-Str. 6-8, 66121 Saarbrücken, Deutschland / Germany
Email: info@lap-publishing.com

Herstellung: siehe letzte Seite /
Printed at: see last page
ISBN: 978-3-659-74863-9

Zugl. / Approved by: São Carlos, University of São Paulo, Habilitation, 2015

Solution of restricted two-dimensional fabric cutting problem

Preface

This book presents the application of a mathematical model in the process of decision-making on the subject of components supply of an APS (Advanced Planning System) production-programming model in a textile garment industry.

The objective is to integrate and manage the manufacturing materials supply from the cutting process, having as a principle the sequencing criteria previously defined in the production programming model. The management occurs proactively, as the programmer identifies critical items of factory supply by making the necessary interventions. From the combination of supply and demand, the production management focuses on finding an overall increase in company productivity both by eliminating the lack of raw material in the manufacture process, and by minimizing the excess of cut material according to standard predetermined cutting setup types.

Key words: Advanced Planning System; Production Programming; Linear Programming; Two-dimensional Cutting Problem.

W. Azzolini Junior.

Department of Production Enginneer, Schol of Engineering of São Carlos – University of São Paulo – USP, São Carlos, Brazil.

Table of Contents

    1.1. Production Scheduling   07

2. Planning and Production Scheduling   09

3. Production Management through mathematical modeling and use of the APS system

                                                                                           14

4. Application of a proposed production programming model   20

4.1. Characterization of the supply process problem   20

4.2. Production scheduler's vision   22

4.3. Queue Based Sequencing (QBS)   24

4.4. Cutting Procedure   25

4.5. Manufacturing process – garment industry   38

4.6. Process Restrictions   41

5. Conclusion   50

    References   51

    Appendix   53

List of Figures

Figure 1 – Hierarchy of planning   09

Figure 2 – Front view of resource – cutting fabric   22

Figure 3 – SMC report the lack of material   24

Figure 4 – Demand for the product group described in Table 2   27

Figure 5 – List of cut material (cut) from drawing the fabric cutting section demand (request the quantity of stock replacement) and stock (difference between the quantity of the default drawing the tissue cutting section of cutting and replacement) for Small size   27

Figure 6 – List of cut material (cut) from drawing the fabric cutting section demand (request the quantity of stock replacement) and stock (difference between the quantity of the default drawing the tissue cutting section of cutting and replacement) for Medium size   27

Figure 7 – List of cut material (cut) from drawing the fabric cutting section demand (request the quantity of stock replacement) and stock (difference between the quantity of the default drawing the tissue cutting section of cutting and replacement) for Large size   28

Figure 8 – List of cut material (cut) from drawing the fabric cutting section demand (request the quantity of stock replacement) and stock (difference between the quantity of the default drawing the tissue cutting section of cutting and replacement) for Extra Large size   28

Figure 9 – 2nd Proposal – List of cut material (cut) from drawing the fabric cutting section demand (request the quantity of stock replacement) and stock (difference between the quantity of the default drawing the tissue cutting section of cutting and replacement) for Small size   32

Figure 10 – 2nd Proposal – List of cut material (cut) from drawing the fabric cutting section demand (request the quantity of stock replacement) and stock (difference between the quantity of the default drawing the tissue cutting section of cutting and replacement) for Medium size   32

Figure 11 – 2nd Proposal – List of cut material (cut) from drawing the fabric cutting section demand (request the quantity of stock replacement) and stock (difference between the quantity of the default drawing the tissue cutting section of cutting and replacement) for Large size   32

Figure 12 – 2nd Proposal – List of cut material (cut) from drawing the fabric cutting section demand (request the quantity of stock replacement) and stock (difference between the quantity of the default drawing the tissue cutting section of cutting and replacement) for Extra Large size   33

Figure 13 – 3rd Proposal – List of cut material (cut) from drawing the fabric cutting section demand (request the quantity of stock replacement) and stock (difference between the quantity of the default drawing the tissue cutting section of cutting and replacement) for Small size   33

Figure 14 – 3rd Proposal – List of cut material (cut) from drawing the fabric cutting section demand (request the quantity of stock replacement) and stock (difference between the quantity of the default drawing the tissue cutting section of cutting and replacement) for Medium size   33

List of Tables

1. Introduction

The main challenge of the industrial companies in the contemporary world is to achieve and maintain operation results accordingly to international standards of performance in a company classified as World Class Manufacturing.

A company capable of achieving such a standard is able to measure the plant performance from the construction of production performance indicators adherent to its manufacturing process, and may possibly intervene emphatically when there are random restrictions that might inhibit the achievement of that objective.

This is done in the pursuit of recognizing both the distance of its goal and the company possibilities of surpassing the level of effectiveness in a World Class Manufacturing company operation.

According to Olhager (2013), for a company to be classified as World Class Manufacturing the operating results should reflect its competitiveness in several areas inherent to the factory operation, which directly impact production performance such as quality, product availability in final customer's hands, cost efficiency and flexibility, all of which strongly influenced by efficiency and effectiveness of planning and controlling the activities essential to all areas systemically mentioned.

Olhager (2013) considers that the greatest difficulty, however, is the fact that planning and controlling tasks during the operation have become highly complex due to the need for shorter lead times, also influenced by minor products life cycles , so that the bottleneck resources should be used more efficiently.

Nyman (2012) considers that the objective of achieving the operation efficiency standard in the levels of World Class Manufacturing companies can be serviced from a structured virtual model of the manufacturing process that should represent the production system in loco, and also states that by considering the interdependence of a number of influential factors from computer simulation as primary resources (machines) and secondary resources (tools, manpower and devices), it is able to reconcile quantified parameters, such as production capacity by resource or production system door to door, drive times, processing times, setup times, and other factors that may restrict the flow of production as to constructive particularities of each product type.

From this tangled interdependent data, APS specialist system identifies the best execution sequence of a given set of production orders, so it meets the requests for the production plan execution in the best operating condition of the system, while respecting the operating rules of manufacture described in the model, in order to completely fulfill fabrication quantities for product as to meeting the due date, which must be observed during operation. In order to meet the statement presented in the previous paragraph, there are cases in which it is necessary, on the part of the production programmer, to use specific heuristic optimization methods. In this case, the APS software, expert in production scheduling, allows the programmer to make the best decisions on what to produce, where to produce, as well as on the quantities to be produced from a finite capacity plan.

Still according to Nyman, if the capacity or the supply of raw materials is limited, the use of APS systems can also help with the optimal allocation of production orders from customers, according to priority criteria defined for a given operation time for specific production orders. The author also points out that by using the notion of constraint-based planning, production orders to be executed can be analyzed according to the availability of raw materials and components, besides the assessment of production capacity in a systemic way, involving all the manufacturing resources in a given manufacturing script, according to the production plan to be executed.

1.1. Production Scheduling

According to Britan (1983), production scheduling deals with the allocation of resources and the sequencing of tasks, aiming at developing products and services within deadlines defined with the customer. In complex manufacturing environments, mathematical production programming models, developed from specific heuristic scheduling and sequencing, are applied through an APS system. This practice has been growing in recent years from the new generation of expert systems in production scheduling, an evolution of Finite Capacity Scheduling systems for APS systems that emerged from the 1990s.

The logic of sequencing defined in the mathematical model implemented by APS systems deals with variables and constraints of the manufacturing process, product mix, strategies to meet the defined demand and production flow.

Products and operations specifics can be considered as attributes, in order to establish criteria for prioritizing the model and allowing the simulation of scenarios for the production schedule.

Apparently complex, the modeling process consists of surveying all manufacturing capabilities and processes of the products to be developed, and subsequent structuring the relationship of all components in the production system which, somehow, affect the production schedule. According to Pinedo (1995), the increasing complexity of production systems has led APS systems researchers to define two steps in the process of simulation in production scheduling as a premise on the development of such systems:

1) The first step is the allocation of manufacturing resources;

2) The second step is the operations sequencing, which resulted in better performance and accuracy in the simulation of such systems. This fact, together with the advancement in hardware technology, has provided users with excellent performance APS tools.

As the problem of resource allocation is solved depending on the production availability and capacity, its results become "inputs" to the problem of sequencing the tasks regarding the assumptions defined by the model ordinance criteria. It is important to highlight that nowadays it is possible to apply APS systems in any of the existing types of production systems. This Book initially aims at studying the current system of planning and controlling of production in a textile manufacturing company, and has the objective of proposing the use of mathematical modeling of linear programming to solve the problem of restricted two-dimensional cutting fabric in the definition of a component supply plan.

This Book was structured in seven sections. In section 2, the basic differences between planning and production scheduling are presented. In section 3, an analysis of the three main perspectives of production scheduling is depicted. Section 4 presents the benefits of production scheduling. In section 5, the mathematical modeling in linear programming with emphasis on solving the problem of restricted two-dimensional fabric cutting and Production Management process through the use of the APS system are studied. Section 6 proposes the use of linear programming model based on the solution of the restricted two-dimensional fabric cutting and Production Scheduling Model for a company of textile manufacture; and, finally, Section 7 presents the results and conclusions of this study.

2. Planning and Production Scheduling

The essential difference between planning and production scheduling is in the vision of task implementation schedule that production plan offers. While industrial planning tasks are contained in overall plans for longer periods of time, when activities are designated for each department, industrial programming tasks are contained in detailed settings for the manufacturing resources in a short period of time; thus, programming allows a high-resolution view of planning (Barták, 1999).

A key difference between planning and production scheduling are the horizon and level of details considered. Typically, the planning horizon is defined in weeks or months and aggregates demand and capacity data to evaluate the impact of scheduling.

Programming, on the other hand, has a horizon of hours or days and considers individually performed jobs or tasks and specific tools, which enable detailed instructions deliverance. Barták (1999) also defines a new configuration for the relation between integrated planning and   program sequencing, according to Figure 1.

Figure 1 – Hierarchy of planning. Fonte: Barták (1999).

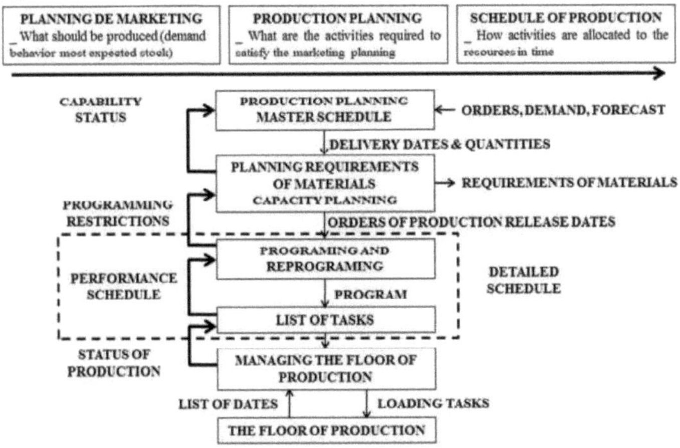

Alignment of Marketing Planning, Production Planning and Production Scheduling, according to a previewed timeline, ensures a master plan for the other levels with a much greater degree of assertiveness regarding deadlines, products and quantities established with the consumer market.

According to Hermann (1983), three different perspectives of the production scheduling previously set normally influence the definition of the model assumptions and should be considered and tested in order to validate the best production scheduling to be generated:

Problem solving perspective: it is the view of the production scheduling regarding to an optimization problem of plant resources. It is the formulation of the scheduling, when there is a combinatorial optimization problem of manufacturing resources, which are isolated, both in the area of manufacture planning and in the system of the factory control. The modeling should consider the variables of the system as well as the existing restrictions in the process of allocation and resource scheduling.

Decision maker perspective: it is the view of the production scheduling as to decision making. The programmer, based on the recommendations of related areas and according to a consensus to be defined by the organization strategy, should establish the production plan that best meets the needs of the company. In this case, programmers must deal with uncertainties and adjust the bottlenecks in order to anticipate problems that may likely occur in the execution of the production plan.

Organizational perspective: it is the view of the production scheduling as part of the complex flow of information and company decision-making process, which composes the manufacturing planning and control system.

Bayindir (2005) points out that modeling, which should support the process of production scheduling, must start from the particularities of production systems, such as type of flow and type of process, as shown below:

• Type of flow

Flow shop: all tasks have identical flow processes and require the same operations sequence;

Job shop: tasks have different process flows and may require significantly different sequences of operations.

• Type of procedure

Processing Unit: jobs are processed one by one;

Batch processing or batch number: a number of tasks are processed in a batch.

It is important to note that there are other types of production systems not covered herein for not being the focus of this book.

The integration, as proposed by Barták (1999), and the proper use of APS systems enable companies to achieve goals with important benefits for the proposed integration from the hierarchy of planning and production scheduling.

A production scheduling can determine whether a delivery promise can be fulfilled; it can also identify available periods of time for preventive maintenance, assertive dates in scheduling applications and a more efficient management of the productive system.

Effective advantages of the process of production scheduling may be related to:

_ a production scheduling that determines an explicit relation of what should be done in the plant, in a certain period of time, thus defining how supervisors and managers can measure the productive system performance, before its implementation, through previous simulations and correction of probable deviations:

    • It minimizes WIP - Work in Process;

    • It minimizes average flow system time;

    • It maximizes the use of the machine and the worker;

    • It minimizes setup times;

    • A production scheduling can identify conflicts in the use of resource, can control production task release and can ensure that the required raw materials are ordered in time;

    • It improves the coordination of productivity indexes and operational costs minimization.

The management of production orders must ensure that subsystems- demand response systems - ETO, CTO, MTO, ATO / FTO, MTS, have their objectives achieved from a program of assertive production.

Pinedo (1995) defines the flow of information and the hierarchy of procedures related to the production scheduling process.

The author demonstrates the necessity of having an adequate and agile flow of information in the manufacturing, so that a production order should be processed by the model based on capacity planning, production scheduling and listed activities as result to the management of the factory.

The production control adjusts the deviation of workload based on factory capacity planning, level of utilization of each resource during production, customers' priority and orders fulfillment, or manufacturing commands, based on due date.

The use of manufacturing resources considers all these factors, that is, the success of the process lies in the quality of modeling that can become more or less assertive from the experience of the production scheduler.

According to the Management process model proposed by Kemppainen (2005), steps must be performed prior to production scheduling, in order to validate both the orders to be issued and the necessary materials from a previous planning including quantities and deadlines.

This is the moment when sequencing is performed and predicted distortion is viewed, thus being the instant of correction and validation before the factory starts the manufacturing process; this is important to avoid work without a feasible production plan that contemplates the needs of the moment.

The definition of the orders, as well as delivery and orders deadlines, can be extracted through integration with ERP systems or inserted directly into the software by allowing, if necessary, the identification of the material restrictions by SMC functionality - Static Material Control, available for the APS version used in this work.

APS can automatically configure connections between different orders downloaded from an MRP / ERP system. The SMC uses information from the MRP / ERP system both to do a product and select the orders and to obtain or provide materials from the structure of the product materials (Bill of Materials).

The link between production orders from the structure of product materials is defined by *pegging* and means that, during programming, the APS will take into account not only the system restrictions, but also machinery and employees, besides the necessary materials (raw materials and ending stocks).

It is important to point out that the use of SMC functionality contributes both in the moment of validating the production schedule and subsequent implementation of the plan, and in the next moment, after the completion of production orders for finished products.

This allows more accuracy in the performance of back- flushing operation of all product material frame components placed below the parent item, not allowing that consumed components in manufacturing do not have their balance inventory corrected for the consumption of these items according to the materials structure of the finished product.

In terms of required functionalities for production scheduling of a specialist software, the APS can be set as "a list generator of structured tasks in optimum way, i.e. by minimizing or maximizing a previously defined objective function, which takes into account the availability of manufacturing resources (machines, labor, tools and devices) and material resources (raw materials, components, subassemblies and assemblies), impacting directly on the inventory level of raw materials and intermediate stocks".

Intermediate inventories are important in many factory environments, where processed parts in a particular order are used for many other orders.

This type of environment is found where the ERP / MRP systems operate in accordance with the strategy of meeting the demand "Make to Stock", applied in the company object of this study.

3. Production Management through mathematical modeling and use of the APS system

Problems related to the optimization of restricted two-dimensional fabric cutting process are considered a classical difficulty of operational research. This is a problem of the cutting process efficient execution, which aims at the loss minimization inherent to the cutting process present in furniture industry, textile manufacturing, mechanical sheet metal cutting and other types of manufacturing sectors.

Gomes and Marin (2012) emphasize that studies related to the optimization of cutting processes are not recent and report that since 1939, when LV Kantorovich studied mathematical modeling applications in industry, an extensive literature on the applications of cutting optimization problems have been developed and published.

For such problems, with a reduced number of possible combinations of cutting process variables and constraints, exact methods such as linear programming can be applied in an inherent feature in the studied cutting process. However, according to the authors, bigger problems involve a variation of the optimal solution search time with computing time exponential growth and exact methods are not able to determine such a solution. In order to support the solution of complex problems, various heuristic methods are proposed in the literature, which can solve a wide range of cutting processes of different types of materials and industrial sectors.

This book aims at solving the case of cutting difficulty which is considered a problem of two-dimensional restricted fabric cutting with regularly shaped convex parts with up to six sides, still taking under consideration that predetermined different settings of drawing the fabric cutting were defined by the company, from the constructive type of their products with the use of fabric. Therefore, it is not the aim of this book to deal with the optimized layout configuration of pieces on the fabric, for the types of arrangement according to amount per size to be cut is a given input to the proposed model, which intends to optimize the time and the number of pieces to be cut from the Drawing fabric cutting types predefined by the company.

The present work adopts as configuration of quantities to be cut by size of finished product type, the options of drawing the fabric cutting types predefined by the company, which were scaled from a model of rational use of cutting plates by CAD software.

According to Teixeira et. al. (2010) classical mathematical modeling to linear programming with emphasis on the problem of restricted two-dimensional fabric cutting is represented by the objective function of equation (1) with the purpose of minimizing the processing time, or number of times each type of drawing the fabric cutting type should be applied, defined in this Book as 1st draft of adopted mathematical modeling, being the minimization of cutting processing time its objective function.

Variables Definition:

i: size of the finished product to be cut. Small (i = 1); Medium (i = 2); Large (i = 3) and Extra Large (i = 4);

j: type of drawing the fabric cutting section. In the studied case, 11 different types of cutting configuration (j = 1 to 11);

k: Color of the finished product to be cut. In the studied case, 14 types of different colors (k = 1 to 14);

p: reference or finished product code that is part of the cutting group type of drawing the fabric cutting section used. In the studied case, 7 references in total (p = 1 to 7);

a_{jik}: quantity of material to be cut according to the specification of the drawing the fabric cutting type adopted by size and color of the finished product (x_{jk} = 1);

b_{jk}: total quantity of material to be cut by color by predefined drawing the fabric cutting type (x_{jk} = 1);

x_{jk}: number of times that a drawing the fabric cutting type should be used, which corresponds to all kinds of possible drawing the fabric cutting sections, a number of folds equal to 60;

x_{jik}: number of times that a drawing the fabric cutting type should be used, which corresponds to all kinds of possible drawing the fabric cutting sections, a number of folds equal to 60, by color;

ϕ: rounding x_{jk}.

Mathematical modeling for linear programming with emphasis on the solution of the restricted two-dimensional fabric cutting section (Teixeira et. Al., 2010).

Min zk = x1 + x2 + ... + xj (reducing cutting time and increasing stock) $\qquad$ (01)

Subject to the restrictions described from the set of equations defined as:

$$b_{jk} = \sum_{i=1}^{n}(a_{jik} \cdot x_j)$$ $\qquad$ (02)

$$d_{ik} \leq \sum_{j=1}^{11}(a_{jik} \cdot x_j)$$ $\qquad$ (03)

a11kx1 + a12kx2 + ... + a1ikxi ≥ d1k

a22kx1 + a22kx2 + ... + a2ikxi ≥ d2k

....

aj1kx1 + aj2kx2 + ... + ajikxi ≥ djk

x1, x2, ... xi ≥ 0, and whole.

The classic mathematical model for linear programming, with emphasis on the solution of the restricted two-dimensional fabric cutting, has as objective function the minimization of cutting process time, which may generate larger volume of cut material than the finished product demand by size, because predefined quantities by size from the configuration of each drawing the fabric cutting type adopted may not match the demand for requested stock replenishment from the dynamics of consumption of each product, which is expected according to the particularities of garment manufacturing segment.

The minimization of cut material amount at the expense of increased processing cutting time, when it is of the company interest, is proposed in this Book:

A version of the mathematical model of Teixeira et. al. (2010), emphasizing the solution of restricted two-dimensional fabric cutting, according to the expression (4), whose objective function is to minimize the amount of finished product in excess, and the group of expressions (5), which represents the constraints of the problem defined in the proposed mathematical model. Variables definition:

b*jk = bmax: maximum total quantity of material to be cut by type of drawing the fabric cutting section given in the mathematical model based on the demand for the finished product by size and color, and the highest frequency of occurrence for each type of drawing the fabric cutting section applied among different sizes of finished products to be cut;

x*jk = xmax: maximum number of times the type of drawing the fabric cutting section is required to meet the higher demand among sizes of finished product to be cut, which corresponds to all types of drawing the fabric cutting sections, a number of possible folds multiple of 60;

ck: Total amount of material by size and color to be cut by type of drawing the fabric section calculated by the mathematical model;

cik: Amount of material by size and color to be cut by type of drawing the fabric section calculated by the mathematical model;

σ: fixed percentage of the amount of product size to be cut by type of drawing the fabric cutting section by the total amount of products to be cut for a specific type of drawing the fabric cutting section;

dk: total requested demand of finished product by size and color to be cut by type of drawing the fabric cutting section.

dik: Requested demand of finished product by size and color to be cut;

total number of folds = 60 folds by type of drawing the fabric cutting section.

Mathematical modeling proposed for the solution of the restricted two-dimensional fabric cutting.

$$Min\ z_k = \sum_{j=1}^{m}\sum_{i=1}^{n}((a_{jik} \cdot x_{jk}) - d_{ik}) \tag{04}$$

$$d_k = \sum_{i=1}^{4} d_{ik} \tag{05}$$

$$x_{jik} = [\sum_{i=1}^{4} d_{ik}]/a_{jik} \tag{06}$$

$$x^*(j,k) = mín\ x_{jk}(j,k,i) \tag{07}$$

$$d_{jik} \leq a_{jik} \tag{08}$$

$$b^* = [\sum_{i=1}^{4} a_{jik}] \cdot x^* \tag{09}$$

$$x_{jk} = \sum_{i=1}^{n} c_{jik}/\ 60 \tag{10}$$

x* is the maximum number of occurrences or type of drawing the fabric cutting section to be used due to the required increased amount of a given cutting size in specific color to suit the quantity of finished product to be cut to a certain color.

The equation notation (11) indicates that the solution to be adopted by mathematical modeling for linear programming begins for each type of drawing the fabric cutting section, and for the division of cutting demand by color and size, divided by the number of predefined size cutting for each type of drawing the fabric cutting section, by selecting the largest value, or maximum value, as the most frequently used parameter of drawing the fabric cutting section type, depending on demand.

Subject to the restrictions described from the set of equations defined as (11).

$$x^*(j,k) = máx\ x_{jk}(i) \tag{11}$$

$$\sum_{j=1}^{m}(a_{jik} \cdot x_j k) \geq \sum_{j=1}^{m} d_{jik} \tag{12}$$

$$\sum_{i=1}^{n} c_{jik} \geq \sum_{i=1}^{n}(a_{jik} \cdot x_{jk}) \tag{13}$$

$$\lim_{x_{jk}=0 \to x^*} b_{j,k} \tag{14}$$

$$d_{jik} \leq \sum_{j=1}^{n \leq 11} c_{i,j,k} \tag{15}$$

ajik ≥ 0, and whole.

cjik ≥ (ajikxjk), and whole.

djik ≥ 0, and whole.

xjk ≥ 0, and whole.

Rounding xj according to ϕ parameter.

If $\phi \geq \left|e(\overline{x_{jk}})\right| = \left|x_{jk} - \overline{x_{jk}}\right|$, rounding up, on the contrary.

Residual stock by size of finished product = (ajikxjk) – djik.

The Table 1 presents a summary of mathematical expressions. The Appendix shows a numerical example.

Table 1 – Summary of mathematical expressions

Color ⇒ k = 1	(i = 1) P	(i = 2) M	(i = 3) G	(i = 4) EG	$b^*_{jk\,(máximo)}$
(j = 1) A710.01	$(a_{111} \cdot x_{11})$	$(a_{121} \cdot x_{11})$	$(a_{131} \cdot x_{11})$	$(a_{141} \cdot x_{11})$	$b^*_{11} = (b_{11} \cdot x_{11})$
(j = 2) A710.02	$(a_{211} \cdot x_{21})$	$(a_{221} \cdot x_{21})$	$(a_{231} \cdot x_{21})$	-------------	$b^*_{21} = (b_{21} \cdot x_{21})$
(j = 3) A710.03	$(a_{311} \cdot x_{31})$	$(a_{321} \cdot x_{31})$	$(a_{331} \cdot x_{31})$	-------------	$b^*_{31} = (b_{31} \cdot x_{31})$
(j = 4) A710.04	$(a_{411} \cdot x_{41})$	$(a_{421} \cdot x_{41})$	$(a_{431} \cdot x_{41})$	$(b_{41} \cdot x_{41})$	$b^*_{41} = (b_{41} \cdot x_{41})$
(j = 5) A710.05	$(a_{511} \cdot x_{51})$	$(a_{521} \cdot x_{51})$	$(a_{531} \cdot x_{51})$	$(a_{541} \cdot x_{51})$	$b^*_{51} = (b_{51} \cdot x_{51})$
(j = 6) A710.06	$(a_{611} \cdot x_{61})$	$(a_{621} \cdot x_{61})$	$(a_{631} \cdot x_{61})$	$a_{641} \cdot x_{61})$	$b^*_{61} = (b_{61} \cdot x_{61})$
(j = 7) A710.07	$(a_{711} \cdot x_{71})$	-------------	-------------	-------------	$b^*_{71} = (b_{71} \cdot x_{71})$
(j = 8) A710.08	-------------	-------------	$(a_{831} \cdot x_{81})$	-------------	$b^*_{81} = (b_{81} \cdot x_{81})$
(j = 9) A710.09	-------------	-------------	-------------	$(a_{941} \cdot x_{91})$	$b^*_{91} = (b_{91} \cdot x_{91})$
(j = 10) A710.10	-------------	$(a_{1021} \cdot x_{101})$	-------------	-------------	$b^*_{101} = (b_{101} \cdot x_{101})$
(j = 11) A710.20	$(a_{1111} \cdot x_{111})$	$(a_{1121} \cdot x_{111})$	$(a_{1131} \cdot x_{111})$	-------------	$b^*_{111} = (b_{111} \cdot x_{111})$
Total	$C_{ik} = \sum_{j=1}^{11}(a_{j11} \cdot x_j)$	$C_{ik} = \sum_{j=1}^{11}(a_{j21} \cdot x_j)$	$C_{ik} = \sum_{j=1}^{11}(a_{j31} \cdot x_j)$	$C_{ik} = \sum_{j=1}^{11}(a_{j41} \cdot x_j)$	$C_k = \sum_{j=1}^{11}(b_{jk} \cdot x_j)$
Demand (*input*)	d_{11}	d_{21}	d_{31}	d_{41}	$d_k = \sum_{i=1}^{4} d_{ik}$
Minimize ⇒ $(d_k - C_k)$	$d_{11} \le C_{ik}$	$d_{21} \le C_{ik}$	$d_{31} \le C_{ik}$	$d_{41} \le C_{ik}$	$d_k \le C_k$

4. Application of a proposed production programming model

The company, object of this Book, has operated in the textile industry since 1921. Currently, it has a mix of 12,000 different seamed items among socks, underwear and lingerie, as well as seamless products such as accessories, underwear and panties. It has two plants, whereas one unit is responsible for manufacturing socks and accessories and the second for manufacturing underwear and panties, which is divided into two subunits: 1) fabric cutting and 2) manufacture. The second plant, with its respective subunits, is the object of this study.

It has 30,000 retail outlets spread within the country (Brazil) per 140 franchises. All that selling effective is served by 130 representatives. It offers the market an average delivery time of 40 days with monthly production plan, with a reprogramming of every 3 days.

The underwear and panties factory has, in its product line, around 1000 different items as to models, sizes and colors.

In this scenario, the company faces stiff competition from manufacturers around the world and to meet parameters of competitiveness, highlighted by Ngai (2013), it seeks excellence in responsiveness to the needs of textile garment products market.

The previously described Brazilian company has two manufacturing subunits, as defined above:

• Component supplier unit: where fabric cuts are made; and

• Client unit: where the reception of cutting unit components is done, so that the production, or manufacture, of the finished product is performed. It uses cut fabric for the manufacture of finished products according to the release of production orders.

4.1. Characterization of the supply process problem

The greatest difficulty in the company is to maintain supply timing between the Cutting and the Making Units. These are two different textile plants in which the first supplies the second.

The Cutting Unit production plan must ensure that the Manufacturing Unit has a continuous flow of production, maintaining the 14 existing manufacturing cells in constant operation.

Nowadays, the low synchronization time between cutting and manufacturing and the lack of raw materials, due to insufficient quantity planning or supply delays, are the biggest problems avoiding the factory to achieve productivity goals.

The lack of coordination between the links in the factory supply chain generates the bullwhip effect, consequently inhibiting the results of productivity. According to Wild (1995), for EOE (stock, operation and inventory) type structure, classification of the company object of this study, with stocks of inputs, raw materials, components and finished products, the operations schedule shall program the three stages of the system that composes this procedure, i.e., the period of input for stock, the production function itself and the finished goods inventory.

While considering that the operations company system, according to the classification proposed by Wild (1995), is featured with inventories at the ends, i.e., in the supply and dispatch, and operates with care strategy demand -Make to Stock (MTS), the model shall provide three levels in the process of production scheduling. As to the input inventory, the EOE replacement structure of this inventory is taken at a rate equivalent to the use of inputs for operating rate, respecting the supply suppositions, according to Table 2, for the company object of study.

Table 2 – Supplier list / item

Suppliers	Smaller Batch	Lead Time
Elastic	500 meters	10 days
Packaging	1000 units	8 days
Sewing thread	200 kg	5 days
Thread	100 kg	2 days
Label	5000 units	6 days
Sweater	600 kg	10 days

The developed modeling shall ensure optimal use of resources, while respecting the constraints of fabric cutting, by ensuring the manufacture lines supply.

The proposed model considers 4 different and interrelated views of the cutting production and manufacturing that a production programmer must have:

• cutting configuration process, according to Figure 2 (combining of product parts to be cut from a specific fabric, involving the distribution of pieces on the fabric so as to having the greatest permitted use);

• vision of the lines of manufacture supply needs as to expected consumption and capacity;

• existing restrictions on the resources allocation and sequencing process from item 2);

• mechanisms for extracting model information, after production schedule programming.

Figure 2 – Front view of resource – cutting fabric.

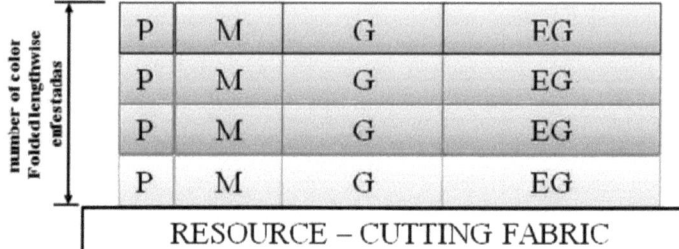

4.2. Production scheduler's vision

The production programmer must keep in hand, from the scenarios generated in specialist software in production scheduling, the cutting plan of the unit, which supplies product parts, and the production plan for manufacturing cells, as described in items 1 and 2.

The model should generate a cutting plan from the types of drawing the fabric cutting section, defined in Table 3, with use of fabric, from the standard measures and based on the size of items, which make up the product.

Table 3 – Options drawing the fabric cutting section

Product	Code Drawin	Width (cm)	Lengt h (cm)	Number of pieces / Drawing				
				P	M	G	EG	TOTA
	A710.01	174	553	48	1200	1200	48	3360
	A710.02	147	837	96	2400	1200	-	4560
400/02	A710.03	146	455	48	960	960	-	2400
405/02	A710.04	147	741	96	1920	1200	-	4080
450/02	A710.05	154	273	24	480	480	24	1440
577/01	A710.06	146	574	48	960	960	48	2880
710/02	A710.07	147	156	96	-	-	-	960
782/02	A710.08	147	209	-	-	960	-	960
784/01	A710.09	147	233	-	-	-	96	960
	A710.10	147	223	-	1200	-	-	1200
	A710.20	157	214	24	600	360	-	1200

For manufacturing companies "drawing the fabric cutting section" means a better utilization of the fabric to be cut through a proper fit in the fabric, thus generating the lowest loss of cloth.

As for the problem of resources optimization in the occasion of cutting, the references are drawing the fabric cutting section in existing models considering the possibilities of size, color, amount of demand (restocking) and quantity, defined in drawing the fabric cutting section, with the purpose of supplying manufacture, i.e., to keep 14 lines supplied according to Table 4.

Table 4 – Production capacity of the manufacturing (garment production)

Shift	Production per production line
1 shift (fourteen production lines of knitting	average 26.392 units
per day (2 shifts)	average 52.784 units
per week	average 263.668 units
per month	average 1.054.672 units
Total – in a dozen	average 87.889 dozes
approximately	average 90.000 dozes / month

It is important to point out that for the problem addressed in this Book, the benchmark group of finished products described in Table 3, there is an indication that related products may be cut together in a single cutting operation, provided both the products color and the construction type is the same, and layout configuration of pieces on the drawing the fabric cutting section to be executed is respected.

Thus, more than one product type can be cut, subject to conditions established in terms of the amount of finished product drawing for each type of the fabric cutting section defined pattern.

From the data of the manufacturing capacity, according to Table 4, and the restrictions of type of cutting, modeling should consider the system variables as to the availability of resources, process times (cutting and sewing) and the existing restrictions in the allocation and sequencing resources process.

The model should generate reports of required materials for the defined schedule indicating dates of use, needed quantities and missing quantities of material to be consumed, so the programmer may follow the Purchasing Department flow of supplies and may, in advance, address suppliers showing critical delivery and delays.

Figure 3 illustrates, as an example, the report generated by the lack of material model in order to guide the programmer on orders having constraint execution in the schedule.

Figure 3 – SMC report the lack of material

Order Number	Code	Due date	Lack of	Required quantity	Quantity met	Quantity unmet
1394	587/01/213	17/jan	1029363	120	0	120
1441	587/01/213	17/jan	1029363	100	0	100
1605	320/02/213	17/jan	1029363	70	0	70
1635	320/02/213	17/jan	1029363	80	0	80
1655	320/02/213	17/jan	1029363	50	0	50
1658	320/02/359	17/jan	1030310	40	0	40
1666	320/02/359	17/jan	1030310	30	0	30

4.3. Queue Based Sequencing (QBS)

The Preferred Sequence rule in the utilized APS software has QBS programming as a "global rule", in which all operations will be treated similarly either to specific product or batch. In this case, a programming rule that mandates a waiting list of one or more resources in accordance with the (s) attribute (s) of the Order is applied.

For the production programming model discussed in this Book, due date, kit control and critical reasoning used in the rank of the resource queue are included.

The kit attribute control criterion is applied only to the cutting process and represents a code for identifying the packet in which the product should be packaged with other models, forming a mix product. The configuration has a pattern of standard mix, as shown in Table 5 (Packaging configuration).

The product column of Table 5 (Packaging configuration) is the probable combination of finished products that may constitute the packing and the column quantity by packing for the total amount of three units, for example, in the first row of Table 5 (Packaging configuration) there are 87 units resulting in 3 kits totaling 29 units per kit.

There are specific instances in which packaging comprises up to 2 products per kit as explained above. This attribute is applied only to the cutting moment to avoid the lack of one of the products at the end of the manufacturing line, at the time of packing the finished product.

Critique Reason is readily calculated, while due date and priorities are obtained directly from the appropriate fields of the data Tables.

Critique Reason is an attribute calculated when dividing the remaining time for the due date by the necessary time to complete the order, noting that the lower the value, the more critical is the order.

The proposed production programming model, from the use of software, calculates the time required to complete the order accumulating a total processing time of the process route. Critique Reason rule is used to minimize delays.

To enable (s) attribute (s) for a given feature, select the attribute in the left column and set the order of the criteria for sequencing the rows through Ascending and Descending sequence.

Table 5 – Packaging configuration

PRODUCT	QUANTITY PER PACKAGE
710/02 - 710/90 - 715/02 - 715/90 - 718/90 - 782/02 - 784/01 - 786/02	87 (29 KITS)
660/02	111 (37 KITS)
400/02 - 405/02 - 450/02 - 546/02 - 575/02 - 577/01 - 635/01	126 (42 KITS)
680/01 - 690/01	144 (48 KITS)
320/02 - 336/01 - 351/02 - 371/02 - 382/01 - -383/01 - 390/02 - 392/02 - 393/01 - 410/02 - 415/01 - 421/01 - 426/01 - 430/02 - 440/02 - 480/02 - 485/02 - 587/01 - 615/02 - 670/01	150 (50 KITS)
923/02	156 (52 KITS)
510/03 - 550/01	168 (56 KITS)
310/02 - 384/01	174 (58 KITS)
115/01 - 155/02	180 (60 KITS)
530/02 - 580/02	189 (63 KITS)
510/02 - 550/02 - 922/02 - 924/02 - 925/02 - 926/02	210 (70 KITS)
222/89 - 274/89 - 282/89 - 284/89 - 290/89	230 (115 KITS WITH 2)
150/02 - 300/02 - 305/02 - 941/01	240 (80 KITS)
515/89	243 (81 KITS)
100/02 - 140/01 - 550/89	252 (84 KITS)
140/89 - 185/89	300 (100 KITS)
251/89	300 (150 KITS WITH 2)
940/01 - 943/01	336 (112 KITS)
160/89 - 165/89 - 175/89 - 190/89 - 195/89	360 (120 KITS)
166/89 - 221/89 - 231/89 - 260/89	360 (180 KITS WITH 2)
942/01	480 (160 KITS)
278/89	567 (189 KITS)

4.4. Cutting Procedure

All drawing the fabric cutting sections of the company are registered in a database. However, drawing the fabric cutting section can be modified or created according to the needs of the company, as each drawing the fabric cutting section results in different amounts of finished products with different sizes (S (Small size), A (Average size), L (Large size) and XLS (Extra-large size), even for the same model.

The record of drawing the fabric cutting section is exported to the developed model. When importing orders, the quantities are generated by product size that must be cut from the drawing the fabric cutting section existing models, suiting the need to cut to the fabric utilization.

The characteristics and configurations of cutting resources (fabric cutting) are showed in Tables 6 and 7, and also the cutting fabric for each cutting resources (fabric cutting).

Table 6 – Characteristics of cutting resources (fabric cutting)

Characteristics	Cutting resource 1	Cutting resource 2	Cutting resource 3	Cutting resource 4
Cutting length	16,5 meters	16,5 meters	11 meters	11 meters
Cutting width	1,8 meters	2,8 meters	1,5 meters	1,8 meters
Duffle	Cotton	Cotton	½ Mesh	½ Mesh
Width of the to fold lengthwise machine	3 meters	3 meters	2 meters	2 meters

On the other hand, Table 7 presents the time of the cutting process. Note that the larger the size of drawing the fabric cutting section, the longer will be the operations involved.

Table 7 – The cutting process time (in minutes)

Code	Width	Lenght	Fold lengthwise	Cut	Separate	TOTAL
A710.01	174	553	30 minutes	145	40	215
A710.02	147	837	30 minutes	145	40	215
A710.03	146	455	90 minutes	75	40	205
A710.04	147	741	100 minutes	125	40	265
A710.05	154	273	100 minutes	40	40	180
A710.06	146	574	60 minutes	70	40	170
A710.07	147	156	35 minutes	35	40	110
A710.08	147	209	20 minutes	40	40	100
A710.09	147	233	20 minutes	40	40	100
A710.10	147	223	55 minutes	75	40	170
A710.20	157	214	55 minutes	75	40	170

Based on data from a company demand scenario, according to Figure 4, models 1 and 2 were applied to linear programming with an emphasis on solving the problem of restricted two-dimensional fabric cutting.

The results obtained from the application of the 1st proposed mathematical model for linear programming, with emphasis on the solution of restricted two-dimensional fabric cutting problem, are shown in Figures 5 to 8.

Figure 4 – Demand for the product group described in Table 2.

Color	Small	Average	Large	Extra Large
111	1390	847	1633	2148
200	1625	1474	2359	1265
204	2025	1521	2487	2613
227	1131	837	1061	707
278	906	1043	1189	1544
359	1353	1160	1282	898
392	557	891	692	1031
434	612	1103	908	228
488	597	1588	692	994
494	851	1373	1141	371
565	796	905	754	1323
784	629	1029	921	447
884	602	792	653	678
999	687	1114	686	1432

Figure 5 – List of cut material (cut) from drawing the fabric cutting section demand (request the quantity of stock replacement) and stock (difference between the quantity of the default drawing the tissue cutting section of cutting and replacement) for Small size.

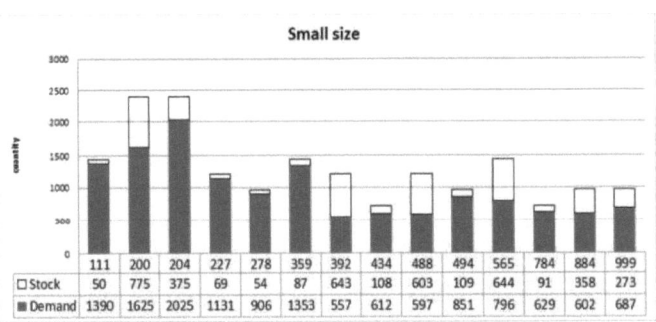

Figure 6 – List of cut material (cut) from drawing the fabric cutting section demand (request the quantity of stock replacement) and stock (difference between the quantity of the default drawing the tissue cutting section of cutting and replacement) for Medium size.

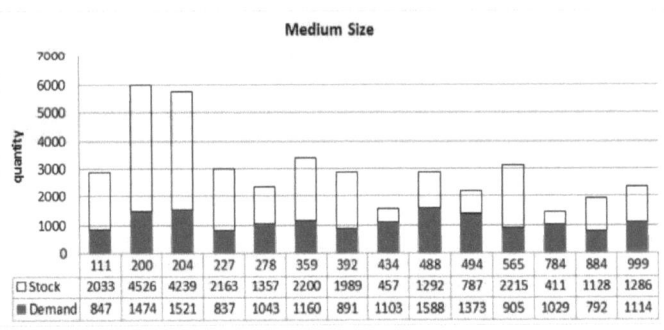

According to Figures 5, 6, 7 and 8, the additional or residual stock is a function of the difference between the demand for stock replacement and standard quantity of the type of drawing the fabric cutting section employed and, in the 1st proposition case, it can be minimized in possible expense of increasing the amount of product in stock.

Figure 7 – List of cut material (cut) from drawing the fabric cutting section demand (request the quantity of stock replacement) and stock (difference between the quantity of the default drawing the tissue cutting section of cutting and replacement) for Large size.

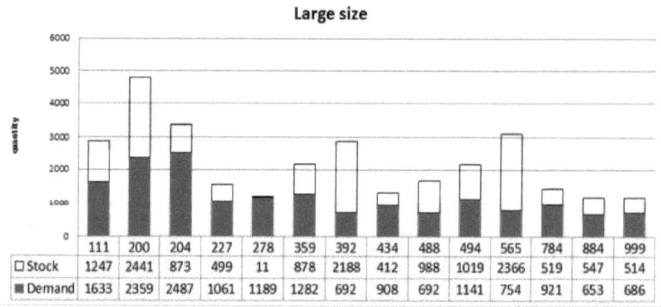

Figure 8 – List of cut material (cut) from drawing the fabric cutting section demand (request the quantity of stock replacement) and stock (difference between the quantity of the default drawing the tissue cutting section of cutting and replacement) for Extra Large size.

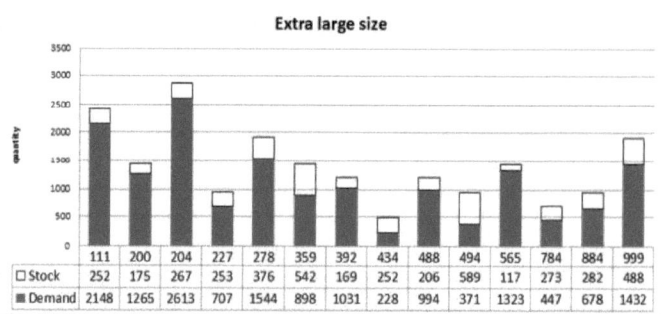

Table 8 shows the results obtained from the 1st proposition by listing the types of drawing the fabric cutting section indicated for each color of the suggested cutting plan from the demand shown in Figure 3, and the results shown in Figures 5, 6, 7 and 8.

The results represent the cutting plan to be executed according to the mathematical model for linear programming with emphasis on the solution of restricted two-dimensional fabric cutting. In this case, the objective function is to reduce the frequency of using a certain kind of drawing the fabric cutting section, in order to minimize total processing time of cutting operation involving: 1) drawing the fabric cutting section; 2) lengthwise folding and 3) cutting of fabric components to be supplied for the manufacture.

Table 8 –Drawing the fabric cutting section options defined by the model for each color of thread (1ª proposal)

Color	Drawing the fabric cutting section options (1ª Proposal)										
	A710.1	A710.2	A710.3	A710.4	A710.5	A710.6	A710.7	A710.8	A710.9	A710.10	A710.20
111						X			X		
200	X	X									
204		X	X						X		X
227		X							X		
278		X							X		
359		X				X			X		
392	X				X						
434						X					X
488		X			X				X		
494	X					X					
565	X					X					
784					X	X					
884				X					X		
999		X							X		

Figures 5, 6, 7 and 8 show the relative volume of cut material , demand or request for stock replenishment and residual stock, from the difference between the standard quantity per size depending on the type of drawing the fabric cutting section adopted and the amount requested, and demonstrate that from the 2nd proposition of mathematical modeling for linear programming with emphasis on the solution of two-dimensional restricted fabric cutting problem, a result in reduced inventory levels at the expense of increased cutting processing time may occur.

It is important to note that the increase in the cutting processing time at the expense of residual stock quantity minimization by product size to be cut is not significant, being , instead, a relevant gain for the manufacturing process as a whole, when the manufacturing process is evaluated together.

In the 2nd mathematical modeling proposal, the gain from finished products residual amount minimization, in an inventory by size and color, is relevant and of operating concern to garment industries.

This type of industry operates based on the collections product mix launched at an average period of three months, which indicates a short life cycle of the finished product and transformation of the remaining stock after the end of the collection in stock, i.e., non-sellable product even with the possibility of promotions.

In this case, the use of reverse logistics as to the reprocessing of these products is very expensive and it is unworthy keeping these products stocked without predictable destination, thus transforming such inventory in a perpetual inventory. The level optimization of such stock at the expense of increased processing time cut, in this case, is strategic and should be evaluated as an alternative to the inherent manufacturing strategy to be adopted for this type of company.

Table 9 shows the types of drawing the fabric cutting section adopted by color and size, according to the results of Figures 9, 10, 11 and 12.

Table 9 – Drawing the fabric cutting section options defined by the model for each color of thread (2ª proposal).

Color	Drawing the fabric cutting section options (2ª Proposal) – φ = 0,04										
	A710.01	A710.02	A710.03	A710.04	A710.05	A710.06	A710.07	A710.08	A710.09	A710.10	A710.20
111						X	X	X	X		
200						X	X	X	X		
204						X	X	X	X		
227						X	X	X	X		
278						X	X	X	X		
359							X	X	X		
392									X	X	
434				X		X	X	X	X	X	
488	X						X		X	X	
494				X	X		X				
565				X		X	X		X	X	
784						X	X		X		
884						X	X		X	X	
999						X	X		X	X	

The 2nd proposition was performed considering φ = 0.04 rounding the frequency of the type of drawing the fabric cutting section. Rounding is a tuning parameter for the important mathematical model on the appropriateness of the amounts to be cut by size, shown from the proposition 3rd, with a different φ for each color (Table 11). The results are shown in Figures 13, 14, 15 and 16. Table 10 shows the Drawing the fabric cutting section options defined by the model for each color of thread (3ª proposal). The obtained result is related to the production plan outlined from a real demand of the company object of study, in the application of mathematical modeling with emphasis on the problems of restrict two-dimensional fabric cutting section.

Figure 9 – 2nd Proposal – List of cut material (cut) from drawing the fabric cutting section demand (request the quantity of stock replacement) and stock (difference between the quantity of the default drawing the tissue cutting section of cutting and replacement) for Small size.

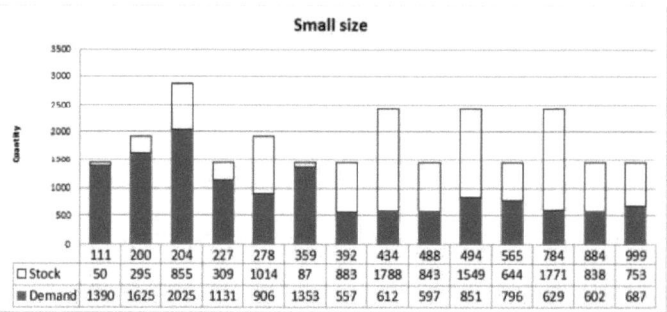

Figure 10 – 2nd Proposal – List of cut material (cut) from drawing the fabric cutting section demand (request the quantity of stock replacement) and stock (difference between the quantity of the default drawing the tissue cutting section of cutting and replacement) for Medium size.

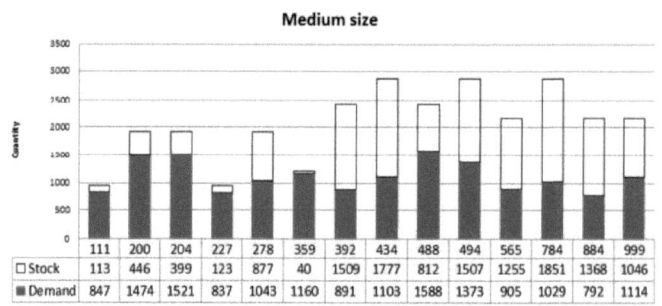

Figure 11 – 2nd Proposal – List of cut material (cut) from drawing the fabric cutting section demand (request the quantity of stock replacement) and stock (difference between the quantity of the default drawing the tissue cutting section of cutting and replacement) for Large size.

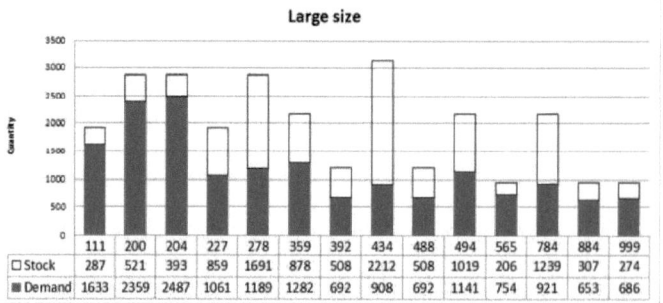

Figure 12 – 2nd Proposal – List of cut material (cut) from drawing the fabric cutting section demand (request the quantity of stock replacement) and stock (difference between the quantity of the default drawing the tissue cutting section of cutting and replacement) for Extra Large size.

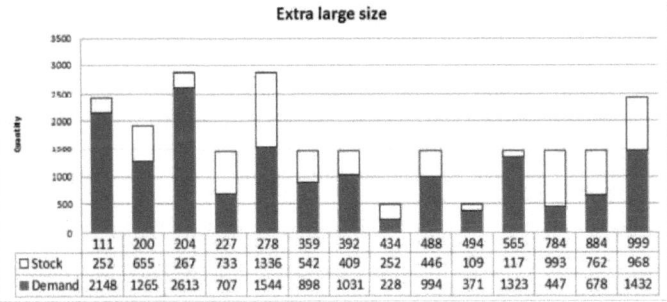

Extra large size

	111	200	204	227	278	359	392	434	488	494	565	784	884	999
☐ Stock	252	655	267	733	1336	542	409	252	446	109	117	993	762	968
■ Demand	2148	1265	2613	707	1544	898	1031	228	994	371	1323	447	678	1432

Figure 13 – 3rd Proposal – List of cut material (cut) from drawing the fabric cutting section demand (request the quantity of stock replacement) and stock (difference between the quantity of the default drawing the tissue cutting section of cutting and replacement) for Small size.

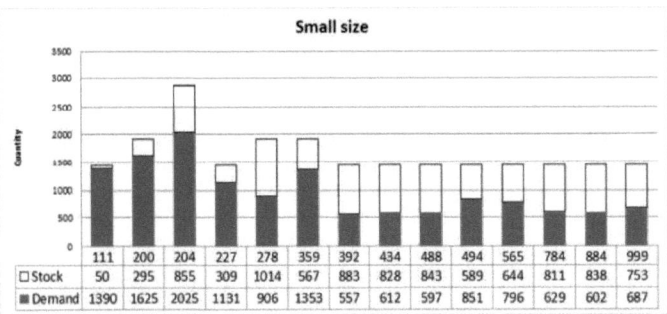

Small size

	111	200	204	227	278	359	392	434	488	494	565	784	884	999
☐ Stock	50	295	855	309	1014	567	883	828	843	589	644	811	838	753
■ Demand	1390	1625	2025	1131	906	1353	557	612	597	851	796	629	602	687

Figure 14 – 3rd Proposal – List of cut material (cut) from drawing the fabric cutting section demand (request the quantity of stock replacement) and stock (difference between the quantity of the default drawing the tissue cutting section of cutting and replacement) for Medium size.

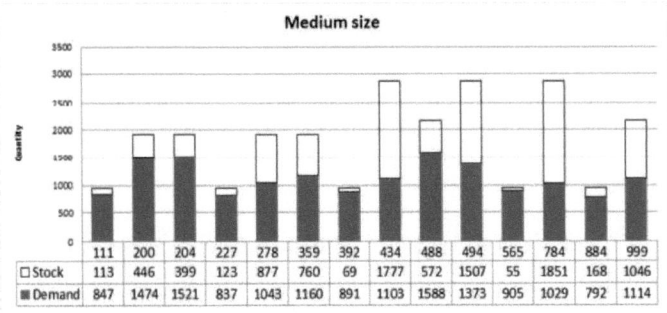

Medium size

	111	200	204	227	278	359	392	434	488	494	565	784	884	999
☐ Stock	113	446	399	123	877	760	69	1777	572	1507	55	1851	168	1046
■ Demand	847	1474	1521	837	1043	1160	891	1103	1588	1373	905	1029	792	1114

Table 10 – Drawing the fabric cutting section options defined by the model for each color of thread (3ª proposal).

Color	Drawing the fabric cutting section options (3ª Proposal) – φ = changed to each color										
	A710.01	A710.02	A710.03	A710.04	A710.05	A710.06	A710.07	A710.08	A710.09	A710.10	A710.20
111						X	X	X	X		
200						X	X	X	X		
204						X	X	X	X		
227						X	X	X	X		
278				X			X	X	X		
359						X	X				
392						X	X		X		
434				X		X					
488						X	X		X	X	
494				X		X	X		X		
565						X	X		X		
784				X		X	X				
884						X	X		X		
999						X	X		X	X	

The demand utilized as database reflects the demand for finished products on a one-week period and may change depending on the period of the year and the product collection. Naturally, the application of the model for a period of time longer than the above simulation mentioned in this Book would be recommended; however, because of particularities of the manufacturing process between the two units: cutting and sewing, it is shown that even without such application, there should be no changes to the results in a meaningful way.

Figure 15 – 3rd Proposal – List of cut material (cut) from drawing the fabric cutting section demand (request the quantity of stock replacement) and stock (difference between the quantity of the default drawing the tissue cutting section of cutting and replacement) for Large size.

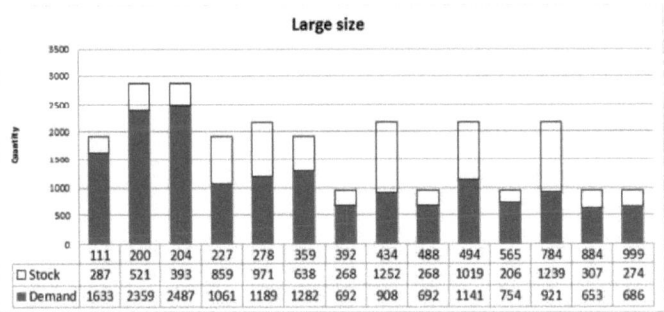

Figure 16 – 3rd Proposal List of cut material (cut) from drawing the fabric cutting section demand (request the quantity of stock replacement) and stock (difference between the quantity of the default drawing the tissue cutting section of cutting and replacement) for Extra Large size.

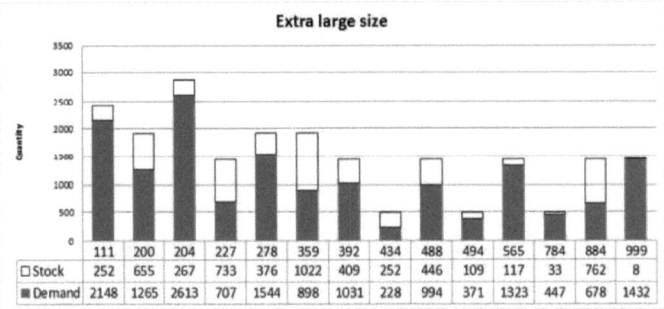

Table 11 – Rounding (ϕ) to each color

Color	ϕ
111	0,70
200	0,53
204	0,31
227	0,23
278	0,09
359	0,20
392	0,21
434	0,33
488	0,25
494	0,32
565	0,40
784	0,13
884	0,25
999	0,20

May such situation occur, it can be solved from the decision making of different scenarios that the mathematical model to the linear programming focusing on the problem of restricted two-dimensional fabric cutting, together with the process model using software specialized in production scheduling can provide. The types of drawing the fabric cutting section selected by color, from the 3rd proposal, demonstrate the minimization of inventory level as the objective function. Figures 17 and 18 show the results obtained when compared to the proposals, as follows:

• 1st proposal – defined as Time (Objective function - minimizing the processing time of cutting);

• 2nd proposal – defined as Quantity (Objective function - minimization of the residual stock from the processing of cutting, according to the difference between the standard quantity per size of the type of drawing the fabric cutting section adopted and the replacement stock demand for finished product , by size and color);

• 3rd proposal – defined as Quantity 2 (Objective function - minimizing the residual stock from the cutting processing, according to the difference between the standard quantity per size of drawing the fabric cutting section type adopted and to the replacement stock demand by finished product, by size and color, adjusting the deviation from the rounding of quantities, defined as ϕ parameter (Table 11).

Figure 17 shows that stock reduction between the sizes of finished product is not uniform and can be observed that, from the proposed 3rd, the stock level is not the best among the sizes S and XL, although the difference with the lowest level is not significant for size XL.

In the overall results between sizes, stock levels from the proposition 3 are significant, when compared to the other proposals, as demonstrated: 32,985 units, against 49,065, in proposal 1.

Regarding to processing time, according to Figure 18, as shown, there is not a significant increase, and in some cases the time remains within the level of other proposals.

Whereas the maximum time reached between the proposals is of 14:20 minutes, the average time of the 3rd proposal between the different colors of fabric to be cut remains within that limit, which reflects a very reasonable result.

Figure 17 – Variation of residual or additional stock

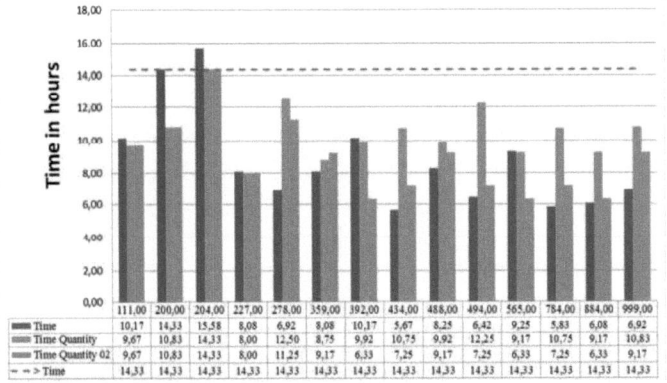

Further variation of the stock

	Small size	Average size	Large size	Extra large size	Total
■ quantity	11679	13123	10902	7841	43545
■ quantity 02	9279	9763	8502	5441	32985
■ time	4239	26083	14502	4241	49065

Figure 18 – Variation of fabric cutting processing time

	111,00	200,00	204,00	227,00	278,00	359,00	392,00	434,00	488,00	494,00	565,00	784,00	884,00	999,00
Time	10,17	14,33	15,58	8,08	6,92	8,08	10,17	5,67	8,25	6,42	9,25	5,83	6,08	6,92
Time Quantity	9,67	10,83	14,33	8,00	12,50	8,75	9,92	10,75	9,92	12,25	9,17	10,75	9,17	10,83
Time Quantity 02	9,67	10,83	14,33	8,00	11,25	9,17	6,33	7,25	9,17	7,25	6,33	7,25	6,33	9,17
– – > Time	14,33	14,33	14,33	14,33	14,33	14,33	14,33	14,33	14,33	14,33	14,33	14,33	14,33	14,33

The impact of this result in the manufacturing production scheduling has been reported from the use of software specific to production scheduling, described in the related processing model of unit operation item.

The model, as described below, has as input the result of the three proposals of mathematical modeling for linear programming with emphasis on the solution of the restricted two-dimensional fabric cutting section, and shall distribute the components supplied by the unit of fabric cutting into fourteen different manufacturing cells, according to the constraints of equipment and labor force.

4.5. Manufacturing process – garment industry

The garment manufacturing cell is the site where the sewed finished products are made from the sales projection defined by the company and held in Central PCP, which is guided based on stock levels and, consequently, on the need for stock replacement .

Some points are fundamental to understand this process and align the proposed model.

• Finished product model: as the company has a great diversity of products, code numbers are made for each of the products relating to the product model, the portfolio to which it belongs (packaging), size and color.

• Product division: the company has 14 lines organized in U production, with an average of 16 operations per line, controlled by a keeper and divided in three factories; each plant has a certain number of production lines producing a specific product range, and each plant is controlled by a leader, according to Table 12.

Table 12 – Type of product per line

Factory	Product type	Line of knitting fabric	Type of drawer and knicker
Factory 1	Basic undershorts (drawers)	LINE 1	underpants 1/2 custom mesh
		LINES 2 - 3 - 4	Basic underpants
Factory 2	Undershorts (drawers) with sewing bar	LINE 5	Boxer underpants
		LINE 6	underpants with silk
		LINES 7 - 8 - 9	underpants with sewing bar
Factory 3	Underpants with bias stitching	LINE 10	Knickers/panties with bias
		LINE 11	Basic knickers/panties
		LINE 12	underpants with bias stitching
		LINES 13 - 14	underpants with bias stitching

• Rates of Production: each garment manufacturing cell has its corresponding production rate determined by the company through studies of timing, conducted in different periods of time. With these rates, the model determines the time when a production order will be finalized and may indicate whether a line needs to be balanced, and also compares if the actual output is compatible with the programmed production, according to Table 13.

The garment manufacturing process starts when the plant receives components, which must supply cutting production, twice a day.

These components are transported by production carts (containers) and are registered in the company system through bar codes of production orders by means of optical readers in place of acceptance; thus, they are registered in the system as cutting orders (specifies that the carts are now ready to provide the material for fabrication).

Table 13 – Rate production

Factory	Product line of knitting	Pieces/hour	Pieces/shift	Pieces/day	Dozens/day
Factory 1	LINE 1 underpants 1/2 custom	220	1760	3520	293,33
	LINES 2 - 3 - 4 Basic underpants	789	6312	12624	1052,00
Factory 2	LINE 5 Boxer underpants	200	1600	3200	266,67
	LINE 6 underpants with silk	220	1760	3520	293,33
	LINES 7 - 8 - 9 underpants with sewing	660	5280	10560	880,00
Factory 3	LINE 10 underpants with bias	175	1400	1400	116,67
	LINE 11 Basic knickers/panties	.375	3000	3000	250,00
	LINE 12 underpants with bias	220	1760	3520	293,33
	LINES 13 - 14 underpants with bias	440	3520	7040	586,67

The carts (containers) only transport cut fabric; the line supplier, soon after registering the arriving carts, fulfills the requests that contain quantities, codes and dates of missing materials requisition and send the rest of the raw material to the storehouse.

From this request, the material is separated and the cart is sent; stocked carts are then placed in a row of carts, in their respective production lines. When necessary, the cart (container) is placed next to the line, respecting the FIFO rule (first one in, first one out), contemplated by production scheduling model proposed from the APS software.

Once manufactured and packaged, the products are sent to the stock. During the manufacturing and review processes, the suitability of the product is checked; as each operation is performed, the fabrication quality standards are analyzed to see if there is anything wrong such as sewing, fabric adjustments , elastic, fabric shade, the position of the label and pulled yarn or scrap cloth.

The manufacturing lines are composed of sewing machines distributed in the cell, at U shape, according to Figure 19, and produce a preset rate of production. Each machine has a function.

Figure 19 – Detailed manufacturing process (Line (05) of knitting fabric)

coverstitch machine	coverstitch machine	Bartacking machine	coverstitch machine	coverstitch machine	review	review
turning and stitching underpants legs	turning and stitching underpants legs	cut and shut the elastic	put the elastic waist	put the elastic waist	inspect, measure and cut	inspect, measure and cut

LINE 5

Uniting the right and left sides	Uniting the right and left sides	Flat Siemer machine	Flat Siemer machine	Flat Siemer machine	Flat Siemer machine
uniting the side right and left	uniting the side right and left	uniting to face with background	sew the sides with side mounted	sew the side of the bulge	sew the side of the bulge

coverstitch machine	turning and stitching underpants legs
Uniting the right and left sides	close side of the underpants - labeling

4.6. Process Restrictions

In the manufacturing process there are many restrictions that affect the company productivity, such as:

• The company production system uses intensive labor force with repetitive operations, which makes working conditions related to the environment such as temperature, light, and other variables highly relevant for plant productivity, for they affect the result of programming based on the model, if an efficiency correction factor is not applied ;

• If the same product color remains for a long time in the production line, productivity is reduced; employees become exhausted quickly when producing the same color for a long period of time;

• Darker colors decrease the production because it is more difficult for the operator to observe any defect in the seam operation;

• Colder weather favors the increase in production rate, and hotter temperatures decrease the production rate;

• The particular operator's experience has a direct influence on productivity;

•More than 50 models of production scheduling system were created for this object of study and each one was developed with a different characteristic. The last three models showed the evolution of software application and have been validated by the company.

The model producing the best result from all programmed manufacturing lines showed a production plan as described in Figures 5 to 8, with the workload for one week, approximately, in accordance with the data described below:

• Resources: The 14 production lines.

• Resource Group: The three production plants, with their production lines.

• Work shift: The shift of three factories, individually.

• Attributes: Only the color attribute.

• Operation: Sewing/garment manufacturing

• Products: All products have been placed with a single manufacturing operation, linking each with its respective factory and production line, according to Figure 20 (1st proposal), Figure 21 (2nd proposal) and Figure 22 (3rd proposal). The result of programming, from the task list, is passed on to the cutting area as a production day plan.

It is important to note, according to Figures 20, 21 and 22, that for both proposals (2, 3) there is a wider distribution of workload among the manufacturing cells than in the case of the 1st proposal. According to Figure 22, the makespan reduction related to the overall manufacturing process, i.e. involving cutting and sewing, is approximately 29%, for 24 hours consecutive days, according to Table 14.

Table 14 – *Makespan* of the three mathematical modeling proposals

Proposal	*Makespan (software)*	Makespan (calendar days – 24 hours)	% (reduction)
1st proposal	10 days 12:35 hours	252,5833 hours	----------------
2nd proposal	7 days 11:21 hours	179,35 hours	29
3rd proposal	7 days 11:21 hours	179,35 hours	29

It is important to note that Figures 20, 21 and 22 (see also Tables 15, 16 and 17) show the supply lines for the specified period, and the time they have available material to keep the manufacturing process. This will guide the developer in case of unbalance of supply.

If some lines have excess material, within a higher horizon program, as in line 10, and in cases when the cutting should provide the supply as soon as possible, such as in lines 2 and 3, the programmer must intervene. It is important to observe that the model does not program orders which have no available material; the programmer can, if necessary, reallocate raw material for idle lines that are prepared for manufacturing the finished product.

The model was developed using SMC functionality for managing the missing materials from data generated by the company system and validated after reports analyses generated by the programming production software. It is important to stress that both color and brand attributes of the finished product influenced the outcome of the production schedule, reinforcing the need to define the specifics of the process and product modeling to ensure a scope of more adherent production plan.

The developed model includes all products and raw materials necessary for production in the 14 production lines, with a production sequence of three operations (Material arrival, Cutting and Sewing), for the finished product , and 1 operation for raw material (Raw Material) which is the cutting operation from the structures of all products.

As it can be seen in Figures 5 to 8, the operations respect the production order (arrival of material, cutting and sewing). Some changes or adjustments were done to the company model, so that fields could be created in order to enable the programmer to verify negative stock portfolio and the type of drawing the fabric cutting section.

Among the developed models, the one described in this Book was the most suitable to the real company operating condition, for it checked all the points needed (negative portfolio, priority application, product color, product brand name and type of drawing the fabric cutting section) before programming the process times properly distributed, pulling the correct amounts through drawing the fabric cutting section.

Data entered in the model were:

Drawing the fabric cutting sections: Drawing the fabric cutting sections were employed, so that the program could associate the drawing the fabric cutting section with the amount of products at the time of setting up.

Stock: As to the stock, two fields were created: one with the stock of raw material, and the other with just the amount finished product in stock (portfolio):

a)   Raw material stock: This field serves only to show the programmer the stock quantities, but it does not influence the programming.

b)   Finished product stock: This field allows you both to perform one of the steps of adjustment, before scheduling the production, and to identify the quantities of the portfolio; the larger the negative portfolio, the higher the priority of the order.

Table 15 –Utilization level of cutting process and manufacturing of knitting fabric resource (1st proposal)

	1 day	2 day	3 day	4 day	5 day	6 day	Sunday	8 day	9 day	10 day	11 day
Resource (1) – to fold lengthwise	78,57%	53,57%									
Resource (1) – cutting fabric	75%	100%	57,14%								
Resource (2) – to fold lengthwise	78,57%	48,21%									
Resource (2) – cutting fabric	69,64%	100%	70,54%								
Resource (1) – separation of parts	50,89%	93,75%	83,93%								
Line (01) of knitting fabric		78,82%	86,47%	100%	82%						
Line (02) of knitting fabric		66,47%	55,92%								
Line (03) of knitting fabric		58,24%	57,71%								
Line (04) of knitting fabric		53,53%	100%	52,60%							
Line (05) of knitting fabric		75,06%	100%	100%	46,82%						
Line (06) of knitting fabric	30,80%										
Line (07) of knitting fabric	64,12%	100%	100%	13,10%							
Line (08) of knitting fabric	55,88%	100%	100%	100%	100%	100%		100%	100%	100%	97,06%
Line (10) of knitting fabric		80,59%	100%	100%	83,65%						
Line (11) of knitting fabric		31,76%	45,24%								
Line (12) of knitting fabric		0%	90%	56,31%							
Line (13) of knitting fabric		67,76%	77,06%	100%	26,24%						
Line (14) of knitting fabric		70%	100%	100%	100%	46,42%					

Table 16 – Utilization level of cutting process and manufacturing of knitting fabric resource (2nd proposal)

	1 day	2 day	3 day	4 day	5 day	6 day	Sunday	8 day	9 day	10 day	11 day
Resource (1) – to fold lengthwise	78,57%	100%	16,96%								
Resource (1) – cutting fabric	72,32%	100%	100%								
Resource (2) – to fold lengthwise	78,57%	100%	25%								
Resource (2) – cutting fabric	68,75%	100%	100%	13,39%							
Resource (1) – separation of parts	66,07%	100%	100%	100%	26,79%						
Line (01) of knitting fabric		67,76%	71,18%	100%	100%	64,33%					
Line (02) of knitting fabric		41,18%	100%	39,19%							
Line (03) of knitting fabric		25,77%	90%	19,51%							
Line (04) of knitting fabric		25,77%	85,29%	4,89%							
Line (05) of knitting fabric		77,06%	91,06%	100%	100%	100%		10,47%			
Line (06) of knitting fabric	67,65%	55,56%									
Line (07) of knitting fabric	66,47%	25,94%									
Line (08) of knitting fabric	48,82%		100%	100%	100%	100%		88,40%			
Line (10) of knitting fabric		67,65%	58,35%	100%	100%	100%		18,71%			
Line (11) of knitting fabric			48,82%	58,98%							
Line (12) of knitting fabric			44,12%	55,99%							
Line (13) of knitting fabric		64,12%	71,41%	90%	100%	100%		36,12%			
Line (14) of knitting fabric		58,24%	100%	100%	100%	61,34%					

Table 17 – Utilization level of cutting process and manufacturing of knitting fabric resource (3rd proposal)

	1 day	2 day	3 day	4 day	5 day	6 day	Sunday	8 day	9 day	10 day	11 day
Resource (1) – to fold lengthwise	78,57%	100%	4,46%								
Resource (1) – cutting fabric	72,32%	100%	66,96%								
Resource (2) – to fold lengthwise	78,57%	94,64%									
Resource (2) – cutting fabric	68,75%	100%	57,14%								
Resource (1) – separation of parts	66,07%	100%	100%	62,50%							
Line (01) of knitting fabric		67,76%	77,06%	100%	100%	13,88%					
Line (02) of knitting fabric		41,18%	100%	13,42%							
Line (03) of knitting fabric		25,77%	77,30%								
Line (04) of knitting fabric		25,77%	51,53%								
Line (05) of knitting fabric		77,06%	96,94%	100%	100%	9,10%					
Line (06) of knitting fabric	67,65%	55,56%									
Line (07) of knitting fabric	66,47%	25,94%									
Line (08) of knitting fabric	48,82%	100%	100%	100%	100%	100%					
Line (10) of knitting fabric		67,65%	48,94%	100%	96,82%			88,40%			
Line (11) of knitting fabric			67,65%	24,76%							
Line (12) of knitting fabric			64,12%	35,99%							
Line (13) of knitting fabric		64,12%	81,65%	100%	100%	34,18%					
Line (14) of knitting fabric		58,24%	100%	100%	89,06%						

Figure 20 – Gantt Chart (1ª proposal)

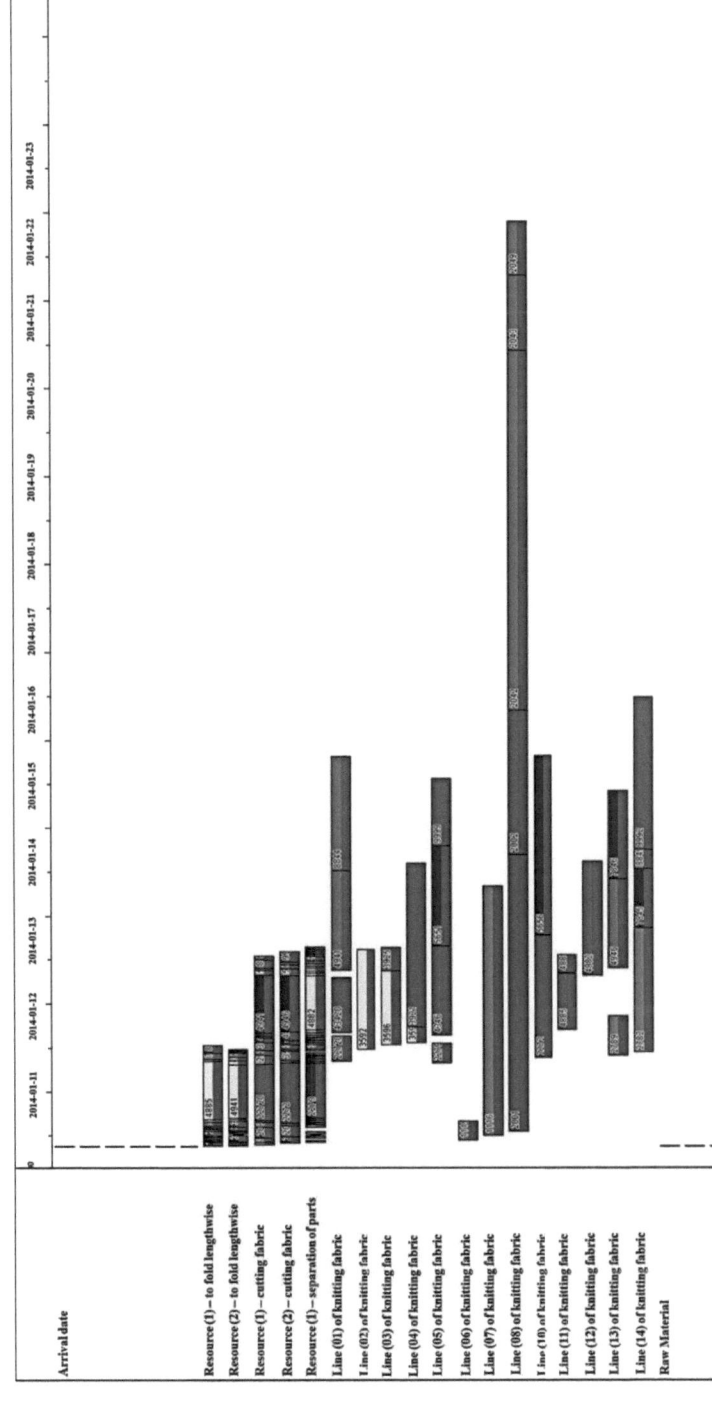

Figure 21 – Gantt Chart (2ª proposal)

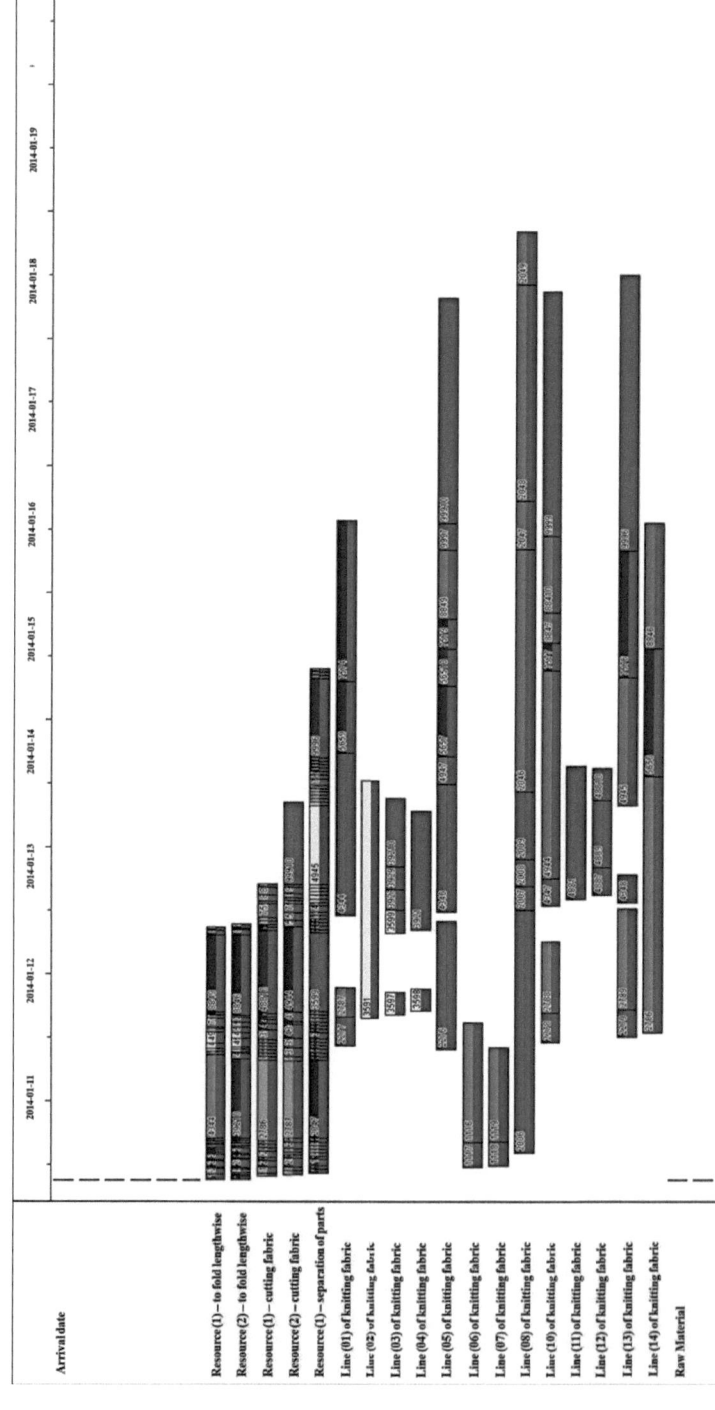

Figure 22 – Gantt Chart (3ª proposal)

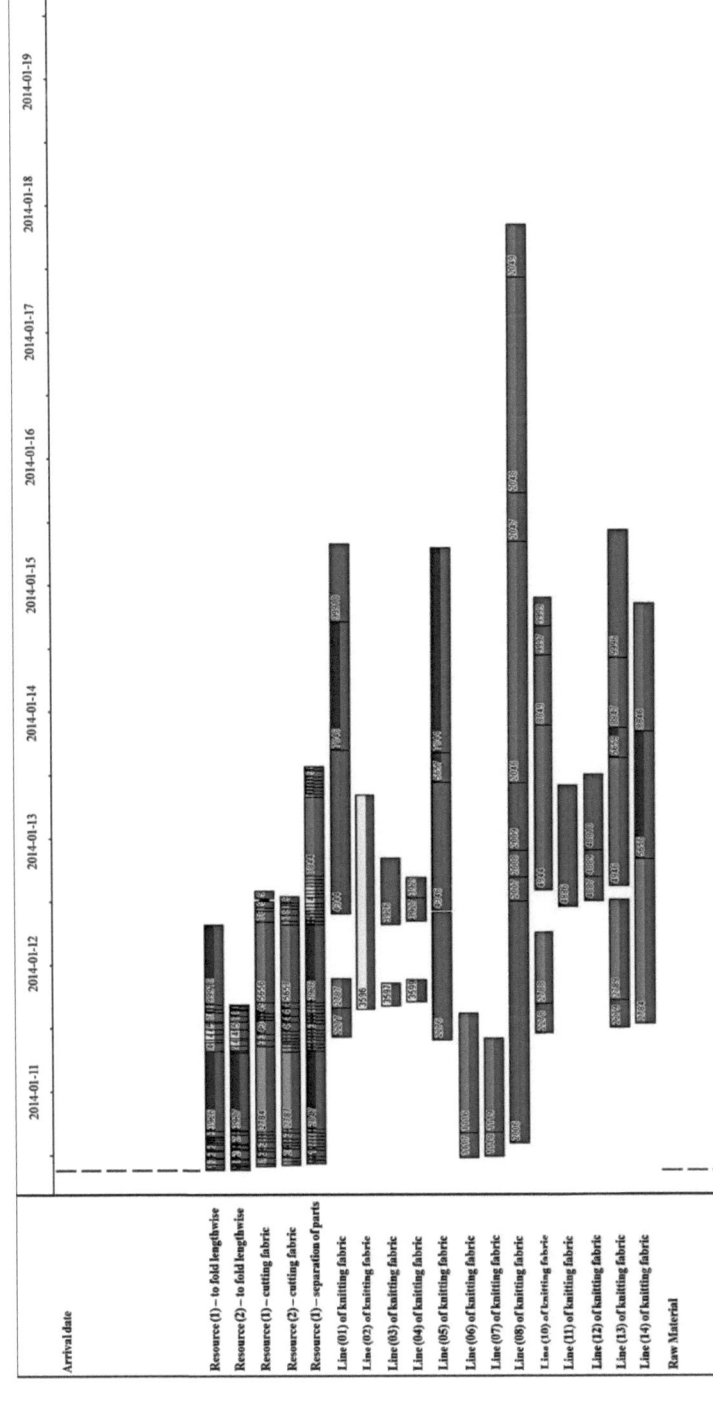

5. Conclusion

The model has not yet been implemented in the company, but simulation scenarios were performed with excellent performance. The effective result of the model application is the view that the programmer starts to have on the flow of materials and lines, in which supply is flawed and, also, as to which items are negatively contributing to it.

Tables 15, 16 and 17 illustrate the use of resources, more concentrated on proposals 2 and 3, with better use of cutting and sewing resources.

The manufacturing environment of textile industry is extremely complex due to the special characteristics of the products and processes involved. However, the company object of study allowed us to assess the practical difficulties of developing a specific programming model of production from a specific production scheduling software available on the market, and the use of a mathematical model to adjust production schedules to integrate cutting with manufacturing process.

The unification of the two working fronts in a research project was a big challenge, nevertheless the result was very positive to demonstrate the necessity and feasibility of automating the process of production scheduling, with the use of professional software in production scheduling, which have reached a fairly high level of maturity as the technology to be applied.

This result strongly contributed to elucidate the company regarding the use of an APS tool, which demonstrates the importance of establishing a common systematic and accurate process for production scheduling in complex environments.

Acknowledgements

This research was supported in part by The Department of Production Engineering, School of Engineering – São Carlos – University of São Paulo – USP, by the Industry Stockings LUPO, by The Coordination for the Improvement of Higher Education Personnel (CAPES) SBN, Block 2, Lot 6, Block G, CEP 70040-020, Brasilia - DF PNPD under Proposal No. 02822/09-1 - line MEC / CAPES "Information Technology for the integration of manufacturing, with emphasis on the production schedule", and by the Company Tecmaran.

References

APS INSIGHT, v. 7, oct 2001. 5 p. Available in: <www.aps.insight.com>. Access in 01/05/2010.

AZZOLINI, W. A. (2009). Tecnologias de Informação para a integração dos níveis hierárquicos do planejamento dos recursos de manufatura, com ênfase à programação da produção, Projeto PND – CAPES.

BARTÁK, R. (1999). On the Boundary of Planning and Scheduling: A Study, Proceedings of Eighteenth Workshop of the UK Planning and Scheduling Special Interest Group (PLANSIG99) Workshop.

BAYINDIR, Z., P. (2005). EIN 4333 Production and Distribution Systems class notes.

BITRAN G. R. A. (1983). Simulation Model for Job Shop Modeling, A. P. Sloan School of Management Massachusetts Institute of Technology.

CORREA, H. L. (1997). GIANESI, I. G. N. & CAON, M. Planejamento, Programação e Controle da Produção: MRP II / ERP. Ed. Atlas, São Paulo.

CORRELL, J. G. & EDSON, N. W. (2007). "Gaining Control – Capacity Management and Scheduling", New York, Norris W. Edson, 3a edição, 2007.

ECK, MARJOLEIN VAN. (2003). Is logistics everything? A research on the use (fullness) of advanced planning and scheduling systems. Book for Business mathematics and Informatics: Vrije Universiteit Amsterdam, p. 1-53.

ENGLAND. (2002). Department of Trade and Industry. Finite capacity scheduling: an introductory guide for manufacturers. London,16 p.

GÓMEZ, JUAN C.; MARIN, HUGO T. (2012). Building General Hyper-Heuristics for Multi-Objective Cutting Stock Problems, Computación y Sistemas, Vol. 16 No. 3, pp. 321-334.

LEHTONEN, J. M.; APPELQVIST P.; RUOHOLA T.; MATTILA I. (2003). Simulation-based finite scheduling at albany international. In: WINTER SIMULATION CONFERENCE.

MILLER, S.; PEGDEN, D. (2000). Manufacturing simulation: introduction to manufacturing simulation. In: WINTER SIMULATION CONFERENCE, 2000. Proceedings.... p.63-66.

NGAI, E. W. T.; PENG S.; ALEXANDER, P.; MOON K. K. L. (2013). Decision support and intelligent systems in the textile and apparel supply chain: An academic review of research articles. Expert Systems with Applications 41 81–91.

NYMAN, H. J. (2012). An Exploratory Study of Supply Chain Management IT Solutions. 45th Hawaii International Conference on System Sciences.

OLHAGER, J. (2013). Evolution of operations planning and control: from production to supply chains. International Journal of Production Research. Vol. 51, Nos. 23–24, 6836–6843.

PINEDO, M. (1992). Scheduling. Handbook of Industrial Engineering (2nd edition). Chichester: Wiley. Interscience. In G. Salvendy (Ed.).

PINEDO, M. (2008). Scheduling: theory, algorithms, and systems, Prentice-Hall, Englewood Cliffs, 3^a Edition. New Jersey.

PLENERT, GERHARD J.; KIRCHMIER, BILL (2000). Finite capacity scheduling: management, selection and implementation. USA: John Wiley & Sons, 251 p.

RONDEAU PATRICK J.; LITTERAL LEWIS A. (2001). The evolution of manufacturing planning and control systems: from reorder point to enterprise resource planning. Production and Inventory.

TAYLOR, SAM G. (2001). Finite capacity scheduling alternatives. Production and Inventory Management Journal, v. 42, n. 3/4, p. 70-74, Third Quarter.

TEIXEIRA, ANTÔNIO C. T; VIANA, DALESSANDRO, S.; VIANA, MARCILENE F. D.; SHIMODA, EDUARDO. (2010). Heurísticas para o Problema de Corte Bidimensional Guilhotinado e Restrito de Tecido, VI Congresso Nacional de Excelência em Gestão.

TINHAM, BRIAN. (2003). APS: Band-Aid or Keyhole Surgery? Manufacturing Computer Solutions, p.10-14, February.

WILD, R. (1995). Concepts for operations management. New York.

Appendix

Considerer the example of optimizing the process of cutting fabric for a particular group of products that uses the same type of cutting configuration of the color $111 \Rightarrow k = 1$. Table A1 shows the standard configuration of the fabric cutting section.

Table A1 – Options drawing the fabric cutting section.

Options drawing the fabric cutting section (total number of products by cutting size $\Rightarrow$ considering 60 folds as standart $\Rightarrow x_{jk} = 1 \Rightarrow a_{jik} \cdot x_{jk} = a_{jik}$)					
Color $\Rightarrow k = 1$	(i = 1) P	(i = 2) M	(i = 3) G	(i = 4) EG	b_{jk}
(j = 1) A710.01	a_{111}	a_{121}	a_{131}	a_{141}	b_{11}
(j = 2) A710.02	a_{211}	a_{221}	a_{231}	-------------	b_{21}
(j = 3) A710.03	a_{311}	a_{321}	a_{331}	-------------	b_{31}
(j = 4) A710.04	a_{411}	a_{421}	a_{431}	-------------	b_{41}
(j = 5) A710.05	a_{511}	a_{521}	a_{531}	a_{541}	b_{51}
(j = 6) A710.06	a_{611}	a_{621}	a_{631}	a_{641}	b_{61}
(j = 7) A710.07	a_{711}	-------------	-------------	-------------	b_{71}
(j = 8) A710.08	-------------	-------------	a_{831}	-------------	b_{81}
(j = 9) A710.09	-------------	-------------	-------------	a_{941}	b_{91}
(j = 10) A710.10	-------------	a_{1021}	-------------	-------------	b_{101}
(j = 11) A710.20	a_{1111}	a_{1121}	a_{1131}	-------------	b_{111}

Demand data by product size are shown below. Equation (16) defines the frequency of use of the option drawing the fabric cutting section based on the standard cutting limits.

$d_{ik} \Rightarrow d_{11} = 1.390 \ // \ d_{12} = 847 \ // \ d_{13} = 1.633 \ // \ d_{14} = 2.148$ (demand for color (k) and size (i).

$$x_{jik} = \frac{d_{ik}}{(a_{jik}/60)} \qquad (16)$$

x_{jik} = number of times using the same Option drawing the fabric cutting section.

Table A2 shows the Option drawing the fabric cutting section for $x_{jik} = 1$.

Table A2 – Option drawing the fabric cutting section for $x_{jik} = 1$.

Total number of items cut by Option drawing the fabric cutting section (considering 60 folds $\Rightarrow x_{jik} = 1$)				
Color $\Rightarrow k = 1$ (111)	(i = 1) P	(i = 2) M	(i = 3) G	(i = 4) EG
(j = 1) A710.01	480	1200	1200	480
(j = 2) A710.02	960	2400	1200	-------------
(j = 3) A710.03	480	960	960	-------------
(j = 4) A710.04	960	1920	1200	-------------
(j = 5) A710.05	240	480	480	240
(j = 6) A710.06	480	960	960	480
(j = 7) A710.07	960	-------------	-------------	-------------
(j = 8) A710.08	-------------	-------------	960	-------------
(j = 9) A710.09	-------------	-------------	-------------	960
(j = 10) A710.10	-------------	1200	-------------	-------------
(j = 11) A710.20	240	600	360	-------------

To calculate the number of folds necessary for each cutting configuration to attend the demand is needed to calculate the ideal frequency xjik for each size and for each cutting configuration according to the Tables A3, A4 e A5.

Table A3 – Calculation of the total number of folds required to meet the demand. Model.

Calculation of the total number of folds required to meet the demand				
Color ⇒ k = 1 (111)	(i = 1) P	(i = 2) M	(i = 3) G	(i = 4) EG
(j = 1) A710.01	$d_{11}/(a_{111}/60)$	$d_{21}/(a_{121}/60)$	$d_{31}/(a_{131}/60)$	$d_{41}/(a_{141}/60)$
(j = 2) A710.02	$d_{11}/(a_{211}/60)$	$d_{21}/(a_{221}/60)$	$d_{31}/(a_{231}/60)$	-------------
(j = 3) A710.03	$d_{11}/(a_{311}/60)$	$d_{21}/(a_{321}/60)$	$d_{31}/(a_{331}/60)$	-------------
(j = 4) A710.04	$d_{11}/(a_{411}/60)$	$d_{21}/(a_{421}/60)$	$d_{31}/(a_{431}/60)$	-------------
(j = 5) A710.05	$d_{11}/(a_{511}/60)$	$d_{21}/(a_{521}/60)$	$d_{31}/(a_{531}/60)$	$d_{41}/(a_{541}/60)$
(j = 6) A710.06	$d_{11}/(a_{611}/60)$	$d_{21}/(a_{621}/60)$	$d_{31}/(a_{631}/60)$	$d_{41}/(a_{641}/60)$
(j = 7) A710.07	$d_{11}/(a_{711}/60)$	-------------	-------------	-------------
(j = 8) A710.08	-------------	-------------	$d_{31}/(a_{831}/60)$	-------------
(j = 9) A710.09	-------------	-------------	-------------	$d_{41}/(a_{941}/60)$
(j = 10) A710.10	-------------	$d_{21}/(a_{1021}/60)$	-------------	-------------
(j = 11) A710.20	$d_{11}/(a_{1111}/60)$	$d_{21}/(a_{1121}/60)$	$d_{31}/(a_{1131}/60)$	-------------

Table A4 – Calculation of the total number of folds required to meet the demand. Numerical example.

Calculation of the total number of folds required to meet the demand (Numerical example)				
Color ⇒ k = 1 (111)	(i = 1) P	(i = 2) M	(i = 3) G	(i = 4) EG
(j = 1) A710.01	1390 / (480/60)	847 / (1200/60)	1633 / (1200/60)	2148 / (480/60)
(j = 2) A710.02	1390 / (960/60)	847 / (2400/60)	1633 / (1200/60)	-------------
(j = 3) A710.03	1390 / (480/60)	847 / (960/60)	1633 / (960/60)	-------------
(j = 4) A710.04	1390 / (960/60)	847 / (1920/60)	1633 / (1200/60)	-------------
(j = 5) A710.05	1390 / (240/60)	847 / (480/60)	1633 / (480/60)	2148 / (240/60)
(j = 6) A710.06	1390 / (480/60)	847 / (960/60)	1633 / (960/60)	2148 / (480/60)
(j = 7) A710.07	1390 / (960/60)	-------------	-------------	-------------
(j = 8) A710.08	-------------	-------------	1633 / (960/60)	-------------
(j = 9) A710.09	-------------	-------------	-------------	2148 / (960/60)
(j = 10) A710.10	-------------	847 / (1200/60)	-------------	-------------
(j = 11) A710.20	1390 / (240/60)	847 / (600/60)	1633 / (360/60)	-------------

Table A5 – Calculation of the total number of folds required to meet the demand. Result.

Result of calculation of the total number of folds required to meet the demand (Numerical example)				
Color ⇒ k = 1 (111)	(i = 1) P	(i = 2) M	(i = 3) G	(i = 4) EG
(j = 1) A710.01	173,8	42,4	81,7	268,5
(j = 2) A710.02	86,9	21,2	81,7	-------------
(j = 3) A710.03	173,8	52,9	102,1	-------------
(j = 4) A710.04	86,9	26,5	81,7	-------------
(j = 5) A710.05	347,5	105,9	204,1	537,0
(j = 6) A710.06	173,8	52,9	102,1	268,5
(j = 7) A710.07	86,9	-------------	-------------	-------------
(j = 8) A710.08	-------------	-------------	102,1	-------------
(j = 9) A710.09	-------------	-------------	-------------	134,3
(j = 10) A710.10	-------------	42,4	-------------	-------------
(j = 11) A710.20	347,5	84,7	272,2	-------------

Table A6 shows the calculation of x_{jik} to define for each cutting type, the total limit to be cut.

Table A6 – Calculation of x_{jik}.

Color ⇒ k = 1 (111)	(i = 1) P	(i = 2) M	(i = 3) G	(i = 4) EG
(j = 1) A710.01	$x_{111} = 173.8 / 60 = 2.897$	$x_{111} = 42.4 / 60 = 0.707$	$x_{111} = 81.7 / 60 = 1.362$	$x_{111} = 268.5 / 60 = 4.475$
(j = 2) A710.02	$x_{211} = 86.9 / 60 = 1.448$	$x_{211} = 21.2 / 60 = 0.353$	$x_{211} = 81.7 / 60 = 1.362$	------------
(j = 3) A710.03	$x_{311} = 173.8 / 60 = 2.897$	$x_{311} = 52.9 / 60 = 0.865$	$x_{311} = 102.1 / 60 = 1.687$	------------
(j = 4) A710.04	$x_{411} = 86.9 / 60 = 1.448$	$x_{411} = 26.5 / 60 = 0.442$	$x_{411} = 81.7 / 60 = 1.362$	
(j = 5) A710.05	$x_{511} = 347.5 / 60 = 5.792$	$x_{511} = 105.9 / 60 = 1.765$	$x_{511} = 204.1 / 60 = 3.402$	$x_{511} = 537.0 / 60 = 8.950$
(j = 6) A710.06	$x_{611} = 173.8 / 60 = 2.897$	$x_{611} = 52.9 / 60 = 0.865$	$x_{611} = 102.1 / 60 = 1.687$	$x_{611} = 268.5 / 60 = 4.475$
(j = 7) A710.07	$x_{711} = 86.9 / 60 = 1.448$	------------	------------	------------
(j = 8) A710.08	------------	------------	$x_{811} = 102.1 / 60 = 1.687$	------------
(j = 9) A710.09	------------	------------		$x_{911} = 134.3 / 60 = 2.238$
(j = 10) A710.10	------------	$x_{1011} = 42.4 / 60 = 0.707$		------------
(j = 11) A710.20	$x_{1111} = 347.5 / 60 = 5.792$	$x_{1111} = 84.7 / 60 = 1.412$	$x_{1111} = 272.2 / 60 = 4.537$	------------

From the results of Table A6 the x_{jik} is defined for each type of cutting configuration shown in Table A7. From Table A7 the frequency method of occurrence is applied for each x_{jik} to standardize the frequency limit on using the type of cutting configuration.

Table A7 – Final result of the calculation x_{jik}.

Color $\Rightarrow$ k = 1 (111)	Final result of the calculation x_{jik}			
	(i = 1) P	(i = 2) M	(i = 3) G	(i = 4) EG
(j = 1) A710.01	2,897	0,707	1,362	4,475
(j = 2) A710.02	1,448	0,353	1,362	-------------
(j = 3) A710.03	2,897	0,865	1,687	-------------
(j = 4) A710.04	1,448	0,442	1,362	-------------
(j = 5) A710.05	5,792	1,765	3,402	8,950
(j = 6) A710.06	2,897	0,865	1,687	4,475
(j = 7) A710.07	1,448	-------------	-------------	-------------
(j = 8) A710.08	-------------	-------------	1,687	-------------
(j = 9) A710.09	-------------	-------------	-------------	2,238
(j = 10) A710.10	-------------	0,707	-------------	-------------
(j = 11) A710.20	5,792	1,412	4,537	-------------

Rounding from the lowest value of x_{jik} based in The Frequency Method.

Hypotheses

The Frequency Method generates from the value matrix "x" (number of times of usage of the cutting configuration) a more realistic pseudo-value ζ. In order to formulate a reasonable cutting configuration.

Description

Step 1: Calculate:

R_j: $1/n * \sum_{i=1}^{n} x_{jik} \forall i = 1, ..., m$

S_i: $1/m * \sum_{j=1}^{m} x_{jik} \forall j = 1, ..., n$

$\beth_{ji} = (r_{jk} + s_{ik}) - x_{jik} \forall j, i$ $\qquad(17)$

Step 2: is $\zeta_{jik} \geq 0 \ \forall \ j,i,k$?

If yes: Stop, the matrix ζ is ready.

If no: Go to step 3.

Step 3: Let ζ_{rs} be the minimal element of the matrix ζ. Construct the constant matrix k: $[_{m \, x \, n}]$, so that k: = $(|\zeta_{rs}|)$ and compute ζ: = $\zeta + k$.

Stop, ζ is ready.

Table A8 shows the calculation of $\sum_{i=1}^{n}(x_{jik} \div n)$ and $\sum_{j=1}^{m}(x_{jik} \div m)$ from calculation of x_{jik} and the Table A9 the calculation of Matrix ζ (x_{jik}).

Table A8 – Calculation of $\sum_{i=1}^{n} (x_{jik} \div n)$ e $\sum_{j=1}^{m} (x_{jik} \div m)$ from calculation of x_{jik}.

Color $\Rightarrow$ k = 1 (111)	Result x_{jik}				
	(i = 1) P	(i = 2) M	(i = 3) G	(i = 4) EG	$\sum_{i=1}^{n}(x_{jik} \div n)$
(j = 1) A710.01	2,897	0,707	1,362	4,475	2,36
(j = 2) A710.02	1,448	0,353	1,362	-------------	1,05
(j = 3) A710.03	2,897	0,865	1,687	-------------	1,83
(j = 4) A710.04	1,448	0,442	1,362	-------------	1,08
(j = 5) A710.05	5,792	1,765	3,402	8,950	4,98
(j = 6) A710.06	2,897	0,865	1,687	4,475	2,49
(j = 7) A710.07	1,448	-------------	-------------	-------------	1,45
(j = 8) A710.08	-------------	-------------	1,687	-------------	1,70
(j = 9) A710.09	-------------	-------------	-------------	2,238	2,24
(j = 10) A710.10	-------------	0,707	-------------	-------------	0,71
(j = 11) A710.20	5,792	1,412	4,537	-------------	3,91
$\sum_{j=1}^{m}(x_{jik} \div m)$	3,08	0,89	2,14	5,03	

Table A9 – Calculation of Matrix ζ (x_{jik}).

Color ⇒ k = 1 (111)	Calculation of Matrix ζ (x_{jik})			
	(i = 1) P	(i = 2) M	(i = 3) G	(i = 4) EG
(j = 1) A710.01	(2,36 + 3,08) − 2,897 = 2,54	(2,36 + 0,89) − 0,707 = 2,55	(2,36 + 2,14) − 1,362 = 3,14	(2,36 + 5,03) − 4,475 = 2,92
(j = 2) A710.02	(1,05 + 3,08) − 1,448 = 2,68	(1,05 + 0,89) − 0,353 = 1,59	(1,05 + 2,14) − 1,362 = 1,83	------------
(j = 3) A710.03	(1,83 + 3,08) − 2,897 = 2,01	(1,83 + 0,89) − 0,865 = 1,84	(1,83 + 2,14) − 1,687 = 2,27	------------
(j = 4) A710.04	(1,08 + 3,08) − 1,448 = 2,71	(1,08 + 0,89) − 0,442 = 1,54	(1,08 + 2,14) − 1,362 = 1,86	------------
(j = 5) A710.05	(4,98 + 3,08) − 5,792 = 2,26	(4,98 + 0,89) − 1,765 = 4,11	(4,98 + 2,14) − 3,402 3,72	(4,98 + 5,03) − 8,950 = 1,06
(j = 6) A710.06	(2,49 + 3,08) − 2,2897 = 2,67	(2,49 + 0,89) − 0,865 = 2,50	(2,49 + 2,14) − 1,687 = 2,93	(2,49 + 5,03) − 4,475 = 3,05
(j = 7) A710.07	(1,45 + 3,08) − 1,448 = 3,08	------------	------------	------------
(j = 8) A710.08	------------	------------	(1,7 + 2,14) − 1,687 = 2,14	------------
(j = 9) A710.09	------------	------------	------------	(2,24 + 5,03) − 2,238 = 5,03
(j = 10) A710.10	------------	(0,71 + 0,89) − 0,707 = 0,89	------------	------------
(j = 11) A710.20	(3,91 + 3,08) − 5,792 = 1,20	(3,91 + 0,89) − 1,412 = 3,39	(3,91 + 2,14) − 4,537 1,52	------------

Table A10 shows the Matrix ζ (x_jik) ready.

Table A10 – Matrix ζ ready (x_jik).

Color ⇒ k = 1 (111)	Matrix ζ ready (x_jik)				x_{jik(minimum)}	Δx_{jk}	Restriction – Limit amount of cut by Options drawing the fabric cutting section Rouding ≤ 0,5 ⇓ (x_{jk})
	(i = 1) P	(i = 2) M	(i = 3) G	(i = 4) EG			
(j = 1) A710.01	2,54	2,55	3,14	2,92	2,540	0 → 3	3 (x_{11} – maximum)
(j = 2) A710.02	2,68	1,59	1,83	----------	1,594	0 → 2	2(x_{21} – maximum)
(j = 3) A710.03	2,01	1,84	2,27	----------	1,837	0 → 2	2 (x_{31} – maximum)
(j = 4) A710.04	2,71	1,54	1,86	----------	1,535	0 → 2	2 (x_{41} – maximum)
(j = 5) A710.05	2,26	4,11	3,72	1,06	1,061	0 → 1	1 (x_{51} – maximum)
(j = 6) A710.06	2,67	2,50	2,93	3,05	2,500	0 → 2	2 (x_{61} – maximum)
(j = 7) A710.07	3,08	----------	----------	----------	3,080	0 → 3	3 (x_{71} – maximum)
(j = 8) A710.08	----------	----------	2,14	----------	2,140	0 → 2	2 (x_{81} – maximum)
(j = 9) A710.09	----------	----------	----------	5,03	5,030	0 → 5	5 (x_{91} – maximum)
(j = 10) A710.10	----------	0,89	----------	----------	0,893	0 → 1	1 (x_{101} – maximum)
(j = 11) A710.20	1,20	3,39	1,52	----------	1,200	0 → 1	1 (x_{111} – maximum)

Table A11 shows a summary of the model's mathematical expressions after the adjustment of the transformed x_{jik} into the standard x_{jk}. Tables A12 to 15 shows the use of the model from the standard configuration of x_{jk} by type of cutting configuration based in the example described on this appendix.

Table A11 – Summary of mathematical expressions.

Summary of mathematical expressions

Color ⇒ k = 1	(i = 1) P	(i = 2) M	(i = 3) G	(i = 4) EG	Δx_{jk}	Quantity limit to be cutting by Options drawing the fabric cutting section ⇒ $b_{jk}^* = \sum_{li=1}^{4}(a_{jik} \cdot x_{jk}^*)$ b_{jk}
(j = 1) A710.01	$(a_{111} \cdot x_{11})$	$(a_{121} \cdot x_{11})$	$(a_{131} \cdot x_{11})$	$(a_{141} \cdot x_{11})$	$0 \to x_{11}^*$ (maximum)	$b_{11} = (b_{11} \cdot x_{11})$
(j = 2) A710.02	$(a_{211} \cdot x_{21})$	$(a_{221} \cdot x_{21})$	$(a_{231} \cdot x_{21})$	-------------	$0 \to x_{21}^*$ (maximum)	$b_{21} = (b_{21} \cdot x_{21})$
(j = 3) A710.03	$(a_{311} \cdot x_{31})$	$(a_{321} \cdot x_{31})$	$(a_{331} \cdot x_{31})$	-------------	$0 \to x_{31}^*$ (maximum)	$b_{31} = (b_{31} \cdot x_{31})$
(j = 4) A710.04	$(a_{411} \cdot x_{41})$	$(a_{421} \cdot x_{41})$	$(a_{431} \cdot x_{41})$	-------------	$0 \to x_{41}^*$ (maximum)	$b_{41} = (b_{41} \cdot x_{41})$
(j = 5) A710.05	$(a_{511} \cdot x_{51})$	$(a_{521} \cdot x_{51})$	$(a_{531} \cdot x_{51})$	$(a_{541} \cdot x_{51})$	$0 \to x_{51}^*$ (maximum)	$b_{51} = (b_{51} \cdot x_{51})$
(j = 6) A710.06	$(a_{611} \cdot x_{61})$	$(a_{621} \cdot x_{61})$	$(a_{631} \cdot x_{61})$	$(a_{641} \cdot x_{61})$	$0 \to x_{61}^*$ (maximum)	$b_{61} = (b_{61} \cdot x_{61})$
(j = 7) A710.07	$(a_{711} \cdot x_{71})$	-------------	-------------	-------------	$0 \to x_{71}^*$ (maximum)	$b_{71} = (b_{71} \cdot x_{71})$
(j = 8) A710.08	-------------	-------------	$(a_{831} \cdot x_{81})$	-------------	$0 \to x_{81}^*$ (maximum)	$b_{81} = (b_{81} \cdot x_{81})$
(j = 9) A710.09	-------------	-------------	-------------	$(a_{941} \cdot x_{91})$	$0 \to x_{91}^*$ (maximum)	$b_{91} = (b_{91} \cdot x_{91})$
(j = 10) A710.10	-------------	$(a_{1021} \cdot x_{101})$	-------------	-------------	$0 \to x_{101}^*$ (maximum)	$b_{101} = (b_{101} \cdot x_{101})$
(j = 11) A710.20	$(a_{1111} \cdot x_{111})$	$(a_{1121} \cdot x_{111})$	$(a_{1131} \cdot x_{111})$	-------------	$0 \to x_{111}^*$ (maximum)	$b_{111} = (b_{111} \cdot x_{111})$
Total	$C_{ik} = \sum_{j=1}^{11}(a_{j11} \cdot x_{jk})$	$C_{ik} = \sum_{j=1}^{11}(a_{j21} \cdot x_{jk})$	$C_{ik} = \sum_{j=1}^{11}(a_{j31} \cdot x_{jk})$	$C_{ik} = \sum_{j=1}^{11}(a_{j41} \cdot x_{jk})$		$C_k = \sum_{j=1}^{11}(b_{jk} \cdot x_{jk})$
Demand (*input*)	d_{11}	d_{21}	d_{31}	d_{41}		$d_k = \sum_{i=1}^{4} d_{ik}$
Minimize ⇒ (d_k – C_k)	$d_{11} \le C_{ik}$	$d_{21} \le C_{ik}$	$d_{31} \le C_{ik}$	$d_{41} \le C_{ik}$		$d_k \le C_k$

Table A12 – Summary of mathematical expressions. Example K = 1 (color 111).

| Color ⇒ k = 1 | Summary of mathematical expressions | | | | Δx_{jk} | Restriction $\{b^*_{jk}\}$ |
	(i = 1) P	(i = 2) M	(i = 3) G	(i = 4) EG		
(j = 1) A710.01	$(480 \cdot x_{11})$	$(1.200 \cdot x_{11})$	$(1.200 \cdot x_{11})$	$(480 \cdot x_{11})$	$0 \to 3$ (máximo)	$b^*_{11} = (3.360 \cdot 3)$
(j = 2) A710.02	$(960 \cdot x_{21})$	$(2.400 \cdot x_{21})$	$(1.200 \cdot x_{21})$	----------	$0 \to 2$ (máximo)	$b^*_{21} = (4.560 \cdot 2)$
(j = 3) A710.03	$(480 \cdot x_{31})$	$(960 \cdot x_{31})$	$(960 \cdot x_{31})$	----------	$0 \to 2$ (máximo)	$b^*_{31} = (2.400 \cdot 2)$
(j = 4) A710.04	$(960 \cdot x_{41})$	$(1.920 \cdot x_{41})$	$(1.200 \cdot x_{41})$	----------	$0 \to 2$ (máximo)	$b^*_{41} = (4.080 \cdot 2)$
(j = 5) A710.05	$(240 \cdot x_{51})$	$(480 \cdot x_{51})$	$(480 \cdot x_{51})$	$(240 \cdot x_{51})$	$0 \to 1$ (máximo)	$b^*_{51} = (1.440 \cdot 1)$
(j = 6) A710.06	$(480 \cdot x_{61})$	$(960 \cdot x_{61})$	$(960 \cdot x_{61})$	$(480 \cdot x_{61})$	$0 \to 2$ (máximo)	$b^*_{61} = (2.880 \cdot 2)$
(j = 7) A710.07	$(960 \cdot x_{71})$	----------	----------	----------	$0 \to 3$ (máximo)	$b^*_{71} = (960 \cdot 3)$
(j = 8) A710.08	----------	----------	$(960 \cdot x_{81})$	----------	$0 \to 2$ (máximo)	$b^*_{81} = (960 \cdot 2)$
(j = 9) A710.09	----------	----------	----------	$(960 \cdot x_{91})$	$0 \to 5$ (máximo)	$b^*_{91} = (960 \cdot 5)$
(j = 10) A710.10	----------	$(1.200 \cdot x_{101})$	----------	----------	$0 \to 1$ (máximo)	$b^*_{101} = (1.200 \cdot 1)$
(j = 11) A710.20	$(240 \cdot x_{111})$	$(600 \cdot x_{111})$	$(360 \cdot x_{111})$	----------	$0 \to 1$ (máximo)	$b^*_{111} = (1.200 \cdot 1)$
Total	$C_{ik} = \sum_{j=1}^{11}(a_{j11} \cdot x_{jk})$	$C_{ik} = \sum_{j=1}^{11}(a_{j21} \cdot x_{jk})$	$C_{ik} = \sum_{j=1}^{11}(a_{j31} \cdot x_{jk})$	$C_{ik} = \sum_{j=1}^{11}(a_{j41} \cdot x_{jk})$		$C_k = \sum_{j=1}^{11}(b^*_{jk} \cdot x^*_{jk})$
Demand (*input*)	d_{11}	d_{21}	d_{31}	d_{41}		$d^*_k = \sum_{i=1}^{4} d_{ik}$
Minimize ⇒ $(d_{ik} - C_k)$	$d_{11} \le C_{ik}$	$d_{21} \le C_{ik}$	$d_{31} \le C_{ik}$	$d_{41} \le C_{ik}$		$d^*_k \le C_k$

Table A13 – Summary of mathematical expressions. Example K = 1 (color 111) - φ = 0,796.

Color ⇒ k = 1	Summary of mathematical expressions – φ = 0,796				Restriction	
	(i = 1) P	(i = 2) M	(i = 3) G	(i = 4) EG	Δx_{jk}	{b*_{jk}}
(j = 1) A710.01	(480 ` 0)	(1.200 ` 0)	(1.200 ` 0)	(480 ` 0)	0 →3 (máximo)	$b*_{11} = (3.360 ` 3)$
(j = 2) A710.02	(960 ` 0)	(2.400 ` 0)	(1.200 ` 0)	------	0 →2 (máximo)	$b*_{21} = (4.560 ` 2)$
(j = 3) A710.03	(480 ` 0)	(960 ` 0)	(960 ` 0)	------	0 →2 (máximo)	$b*_{31} = (2.400 ` 2)$
(j = 4) A710.04	(960 ` 0)	(1.920 ` 0)	(1.200 ` 0)	------	0 →2 (máximo)	$b*_{41} = (4.080 ` 2)$
(j = 5) A710.05	(240 ` 0)	(480 ` 0)	(480 ` 0)	(240 ` 0)	0 →1 (máximo)	$b*_{51} = (1.440 ` 1)$
(j = 6) A710.06	(480 ` 0,88)	(960 ` 0,88)	(960 ` 0,88)	(480 ` 0,88)	0 →2 (máximo)	$b*_{61} = (2.880 ` 2)$
(j = 7) A710.07	(960 ` 1,01)	------	------	------	0 →3 (máximo)	$b*_{71} = (960 ` 3)$
(j = 8) A710.08	------	------	(960 ` 0,82)	------	0 →2 (máximo)	$b*_{81} = (960 ` 2)$
(j = 9) A710.09	------	------	------	(960 ` 1,8)	0 →5 (máximo)	$b*_{91} = (960 ` 5)$
(j = 10) A710.10	------	(1.200 ` 0)	------	------	0 →1 (máximo)	$b*_{101} = (1.200 ` 1)$
(j = 11) A710.20	(240 ` 0)	(600 ` 0)	(360 ` 0)	------	0 →1 (máximo)	$b*_{111} = (1.200 ` 1)$
Total	$C_{ik} = \sum_{j=1}^{11}(a_{j11} \cdot x_{jk})$	$C_{ik} = \sum_{j=1}^{11}(a_{j21} \cdot x_{jk})$	$C_{ik} = \sum_{j=1}^{11}(a_{j31} \cdot x_{jk})$	$C_{ik} = \sum_{j=1}^{11}(a_{j41} \cdot x_{jk})$		$C_k = \sum_{j=1}^{11}(b_{jk}^* \cdot x_{jk}^*)$
Demand (input)	d_{11}	d_{21}	d_{31}	d_{41}		$d_k^* = \sum_{i=1}^{4} d_{ik}$
Minimize ⇒ $(d_{ik} - C_k)$	$d_{11} \leq C_{ik}$	$d_{21} \leq C_{ik}$	$d_{31} \leq C_{ik}$	$d_{41} \leq C_{ik}$		$d_k^* \leq C_k$

Table A14 – Summary of model's mathematical expressions. Example K = 1 (color 111)- ϕ = 0,796.

Color ⇒ k = 1	Summary of model's mathematical expressions – ϕ = 0,796				Δx_{jk}	Restriction $\{b^*_{jk}\}$
	(i = 1) P	(i = 2) M	(i = 3) G	(i = 4) EG		
(j = 1) A710.01	(0)	(0)	(0)	(0)	0 ≤	b^*_{11} = (10.080)
(j = 2) A710.02	(0)	(0)	(0)	-------	0 ≤	b^*_{21} = (9.120)
(j = 3) A710.03	(0)	(0)	(0)	-------	0 ≤	b^*_{31} = (4.800)
(j = 4) A710.04	(0)	(0)	(0)	-------	0 ≤	b^*_{41} = (8.160)
(j = 5) A710.05	(0)	(0)	(0)	(0)	0 ≤	b^*_{51} = (1.440)
(j = 6) A710.06	(422,4)	(844,8)	(844,8)	(422,4)	2534,4 ≤	b^*_{61} = (5.760)
(j = 7) A710.07	(969,6)	-------	-------	-------	969,6 ≤	b^*_{71} = (2.880)
(j = 8) A710.08	-------	-------	(787,2)	-------	787,2 ≤	b^*_{81} = (1.920)
(j = 9) A710.09	-------	-------	-------	(1.728)	0 ≤	b^*_{91} = (4.800)
(j = 10) A710.10	-------	(0)	-------	-------	0 ≤	b^*_{101} = (1.200)
(j = 11) A710.20	(0)	(0)	(0)	-------	0 ≤	b^*_{111} = (1.200)
Total	C_{ik} = 1.392	C_{ik} = 844,8	C_{ik} = 1.632	C_{ik} = 2.150,4	6.019,2 ≤	C_k = 51.360
Demand (*input*)	1.390	847	1.633	2.148	6.019,2 ≥	d^*_k = 6.018
Minimize ⇒ (d_{ik} – C_k)	1.390 ≤ 1.392	847 ≥ 844,8	1.633 ≥ 1.632	2.148 ≤ 2.150,4	6.019,2 ≤ 51.360	6.018 ≤ 51.360

Table A15 – Summary of mathematical expressions. Example K = 1 (color 111) – φ = 0,796. Rounding of x_{jk}.

Color ⇒ k = 1	Summary of mathematical expressions – φ = 0,796 – Rounding of x_{jk}				Δx_{jk}	Rounding [b*$_{jk}$]
	(i = 1) P	(i = 2) M	(i = 3) G	(i = 4) EG		
(j = 1) A710.01	(0)	(0)	(0)	(0)	0 ≤	b*$_{11}$ = (10.080)
(j = 2) A710.02	(0)	(0)	(0)	--------	0 ≤	b*$_{21}$ = (9.120)
(j = 3) A710.03	(0)	(0)	(0)	--------	0 ≤	b*$_{31}$ = (4.800)
(j = 4) A710.04	(0)	(0)	(0)	--------	0 ≤	b*$_{41}$ = (8.160)
(j = 5) A710.05	(0)	(0)	(0)	(0)	0 ≤	b*$_{51}$ = (1.440)
(j = 6) A710.06	(480 ` 1 = 480)	(960 ` 1 = 960)	(960 ` 1 = 960)	(480 ` 1 = 480)	2534,4 ≤	b*$_{61}$ = (5.760)
(j = 7) A710.07	(960 ` 1 = 960)	--------	--------	--------	969,6 ≤	b*$_{71}$ = (2.880)
(j = 8) A710.08	--------	--------	(960 ` 1 = 960)	--------	787,2 ≤	b*$_{81}$ = (1.920)
(j = 9) A710.09	--------	--------	--------	(960 ` 2 = 1.920)	0 ≤	b*$_{91}$ = (4.800)
(j = 10) A710.10	--------	(0)	--------	--------	0 ≤	b*$_{101}$ = (1.200)
(j = 11) A710.20	(0)	(0)	(0)	--------	0 ≤	b*$_{111}$ = (1.200)
Total	C_{ik} = 1.440	C_{ik} = 960	C_{ik} = 1.920	C_{ik} = 2.400	6.720≤	C_k = 51.360
Demand (*input*)	1.390	847	1.633	2.148	6.720≥	$d*_k$ = 6.018
Minimize ⇒ ($d_{ik} - C_k$)	1.390≤1.440	847≤960	1.633≤1.920	2.148 ≤ 2.400	6.720≤ 51.360	6.018≤ 51.360
Stock cutting product ($d_{ik} - C_k$)	- 50	- 113	- 287	- 252		

The result is the minimization of the difference ($d_{ik} - c_k$) according to the results of Table A15.

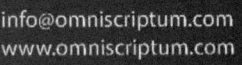